always up to date

The law changes, but Nolo is always on top of it! We offer several ways to make sure you and your Nolo products are always up to date:

1 **Nolo's Legal Updater**
We'll send you an email whenever a new edition of your book is published! Sign up at **www.nolo.com/legalupdater**.

2 **Updates @ Nolo.com**
Check **www.nolo.com/update** to find recent changes in the law that affect the current edition of your book.

3 **Nolo Customer Service**
To make sure that this edition of the book is the most recent one, call us at **800-728-3555** and ask one of our friendly customer service representatives.
Or find out at **www.nolo.com**.

D1504890

JUL   2005

please note

We believe accurate and current legal information should help you solve many of your own legal problems on a cost-efficient basis. But this text is not a substitute for personalized advice from a knowledgeable lawyer. If you want the help of a trained professional, consult an attorney licensed to practice in your state.

1st edition

All I Need Is Money

How to Finance Your Invention

by Jack Lander

FIRST EDITION   MAY 2005

Editor   RICH STIM

Book & Cover Design TERRI HEARSH

Proofreading   JOE SADUSKY

Index   BAYSIDE INDEXING SERVICE

Printing   CONSOLIDATED PRINTERS, INC.

Lander, Jack.
   All I Need is money : how to finance your invention / by Jack Lander.--1st ed.
    p.cm.
  ISBN 1-4133-00190-8 (alk. paper)
   1. New products. I. New products--Marketing. 3. Inventions--Finance. 4. Venture
capital. I. Title.

  HF5415.153.L36 2005
  658.15'224--dc22

                                          2005043093

Quantity sales: For information on bulk purchases or corporate premium sales, please contact the Special Sales Department. For academic sales or textbook adoptions, ask for Academic Sales. Call 800-955-4775 or write to Nolo, 950 Parker Street, Berkeley, CA 94710.

Acknowledgments

Thanks to:

Dick Morley, the father of the Programmable Logic Controller (industrial counterpart to the personal computer), who contributed excellent advice from the perspective of the seasoned inventor, entrepreneur, and angel.

Joanne Hayes-Rines, publisher of *Inventors' Digest*, who, through her excellent magazine, has made innumerable indirect contributions to this book and to the field of inventing in general.

Jim White, author of *Will It Sell?*, who provided several suggestions that add much to this book.

Andy Gibbs, CEO of PatentCafe, who contributed a number of helpful concepts and resources.

And Wendy Hile, Mr. Dickinson's secretary, who coordinated the foreword.

Dedication

This book is dedicated to every inventor who has the will but is uncertain of the way.

Foreword

As a former Director of the U.S. Patent and Trademark Office and a practicing patent attorney, I know first-hand the challenges inventors and entrepreneurs face in bringing their inventions and business ideas to reality, especially when it comes to securing the capital and other resources they need to make their dreams a commercial success. Jack Lander has done us all a great service in setting down clearly and pragmatically the issues inventors and developers face and the steps they need to take to bring those great ideas to market.

While this is rarely a quick or easy process, the message here is that it can be done, and this volume is an excellent source of guidance on just how to do it. In succinct fashion, Jack deals with a number of the critical issues in the financing and commercialization process, including creating a business plan and developing sources of funding and partnering. Anyone considering embarking on this greatest of journeys will find much to admire in this volume.

Q. Todd Dickinson
Former Under Secretary of Commerce for
Intellectual Property and Director of the
United States Patent and Trademark Office

Table of Contents

4 Self-Financing Your Idea

5 Lenders and Investors

6 Communicating Your Ideas

7 Preparing Your Business Proposal or Business Plan

12 Resources

The Money Hierarchy

In this book I will explain how to find the money necessary to empower your dream. The challenge of acquiring financial sponsorship for your great idea can be broken into three questions:

- How much money do you need to successfully commercialize your invention?
- How do you locate people willing to lend money for or invest money in your invention's potential?
- What are the objectives of the lenders and investors, and how can you meet them?

Throughout this book I will address these questions, but always keep in mind that no one—neither investor nor customers—will seek you out. Thomas Watson, the man who created IBM, once said, "IBM products are sold, not bought." This book will show you how to "sell" your invention and hopefully make the journey from idea to commercialization pleasant and rewarding.

You may find the path to successful inventing discouraging at times. Not every invention story has a happy ending. I say this based on my years of experience, observation, teaching, and writing in this field. In general, I am an optimist, and I consider myself successful as an inventor with many patents.

In the end, I think that you will feel good about what I have told you—

encouraged to go on and create. And hopefully you will find support, both moral and financial, and even make money if that is your objective.

This chapter is devoted to the first step: familiarizing yourself with the sources of potential income, or what I call the money hierarchy.

Let's start the process by visualizing the sources of money utilized by inventors as a hierarchy—that is, a succession of steps with you starting solo at the bottom, and working your way upwards (See Illustration 1, below). You may not need to progress far to reach success. For example, inventors who license an invention (inventors-for-royalties) commonly stop after the first or second step in the hierarchy.

It's also likely that you won't need all the types of financing. For example, few inventors progress to the public offering stage, and some inventors manufacture a product and bring it to market (I'll call these "entrepreneurial inventors") with the help of a single investor (which I sometimes refer to as "angel investors.")

The principle underlying the money hierarchy is clear: Products evolve from inventions; inventions evolve from ideas; and each stage of evolution is increasingly expensive. Each of the steps and forms of financing, below, is discussed in detail later in this book.

Money Hierarchy

Step 1: Gas Money

Gas money is out-of-pocket expenses used to record your great idea, assess its marketability, and obtain a patent search.

Step 2: Seed Money

Seed money may come from out-of-pocket financing or may come from family and friends. It's used to make a prototype of your invention, file for a utility patent, or license your invention.

Step 3: Angel Finance

Angel finance refers to private investors: individuals who pay for professional design, tooling, and test marketing of your product. An angel may also finance increases in production.

Step 4: Bank Loans and Venture Capital

These institutional lenders and investors bankroll major production roll-outs, expanded product lines, and more extensive marketing efforts. Institutional investment is also used to prepare for the initial public offering.

Step 5: The IPO

The initial public offering is the final financing step and is used to complete financing and to reward early investors.

Gas Money [$500 to $1,250]

Most of the terminology I use—for example, seed money, angel finance, and venture capital—is well-known among those seeking finance. I created the term "gas money" as my way of saying that you will need "fuel" to drive to the "seed store" (or maybe several seed stores, because the first few may refuse your business).

You'll use gas money primarily to pay for a marketability study to determine the likelihood of commercial success and for a patent search to determine the likelihood of qualifying for a patent. You should not skip the marketability study; it may convince you to stop working on one invention and start on something new, thereby saving you thousands of dollars. The source for gas money is commonly your personal finances.

Seed Money [$7,000 to $15,000]

Seed money is commonly used to design your future product, make a prototype, and protect the invention with a utility patent. Be prepared; the prototype expenses may balloon if your invention is complicated—for example, an electro-mechanical device prototype may exceed $35,000. Sometimes seed money is also used to create a business entity—for example, to form a corporation—that will own the invention and will solicit investors. The source for seed money is either your personal finance or loans or investments from friends and family.

Angel Finance [$25,000 to $1,000,000]

Angel financing refers to private financing, specifically individuals willing to finance speculative ventures with higher-than-usual risk. (The term "angel" originated on Broadway to cover investors in stage shows, which are almost always high-risk ventures.)

Angel finance is often used to finance the design of the product—that is, its appearance, function, and design for economic manufacturing—and to obtain more patent protection if possible. Angels may also finance the protection and exploitation of a trademark—the name or logo that signifies your invention or business—or they may underwrite initial production and marketing expenses.

Many angels have started or bought into businesses, built them to a high level of success, and sold them to a larger corporation or "taken them public" (transformed them to a corporation

having stock that can be publicly traded) and cashed out. Others are talented retired executives who want to "stay in the game." Usually, they become directly or indirectly involved in the management of your venture and help to drive it towards success.

Venture Capital and Bank Loans [$50,000 to $10,000,000]

Venture capital and bank loans are used for many entrepreneurial purposes, commonly to expand marketing efforts, increase production, expand product lines, and increase territory. Institutional investment is also used to prepare for the initial public offering.

I have grouped venture capital and bank loans together because they represent institutional lenders and investors rather than the private financing of angels, friends, or family. An entrepreneurial inventor may use one or both of these sources of institutional finance to take the fledgling business to full national and international marketing, add to the product line, and possibly finance the IPO (initial public offering of stock). In cases of both venture capital and bank loans, an experienced business team must be in place either to attract the investment or as a condition of the institutional funding.

There are obvious dissimilarities between bank loans and venture capital.

Acquiring bank loans requires credit history, business experience, and some source of collateral to guarantee the loan. Venture capital—cash investments from investment companies—is granted selectively and is more likely to go to businesses based on patented technology products or methods.

Initial Public Offerings (IPOs) [$1,000,000 and above]

IPOs are legendary for making millionaires out of company secretaries, but they're also difficult to achieve and are probably used by only a small fraction of those who acquire a patent. An IPO is a company's first sale of stock to the public and is also referred to as "going public." As a result of an IPO, a company receives a large cash infusion and is listed on a stock exchange, and the public may buy and sell shares of the company.

Plans Are Useless

President Dwight D. Eisenhower once said that, "Plans are nothing; planning is everything." In other words, we can't always predict the destiny of our great ideas, and we must remain receptive to changes along the way. The changes are not always to the invention itself; they may be in the way we profit from it. We may acquire partners along the way due to convenience, efficiency, or even necessity. Or we may start out to form a small company and produce the invention, and end up licensing it. In short, plan to be flexible as you pursue invention financing.

Chapter 2

Will You License or Manufacture?

This chapter is devoted to helping you determine whether you want to license or manufacture your great idea—a decision that will affect how much money you need and from whom you should solicit the money. (If you've already made that decision, proceed to Chapter 3 to learn how to define and develop your idea.)

If you are a typical inventor, you will probably want to license your invention and collect royalties, or even sell it outright—I'll call this person the "inventor-for-royalties." Licensing is a simpler, less-expensive route than manufacturing and selling your invention. All you'll need is to find the right people to review your great idea and provide the money necessary to develop, protect, and make it marketable.

If you are more motivated and have a competitive business streak—I'll call this person the "entrepreneurial inventor"—you may wish to start a small business to produce your invention and market it. In that case, this book will help you find the financing necessary to develop, produce, and distribute your product. Entrepreneurial inventors become involved in more complex financing than an inventor-for-royalties—for example, selling shares of stock (or other interests) in the business and invention.

To some extent, your decision is influenced by your invention. Certain innovations, because of their complexity, scope, or exorbitant cost of production, may lend themselves to licensing. Often, however, the decision is based much more on you than on your invention. You must objectively examine your inventing personality.

In dealing with hundreds of inventors over many years, being an inventor myself, and having two close friends who are extraordinary inventors (geniuses, in my opinion), I have come to know the extremes of the inventor personality very well. Think of the inventor personality as a set of scales: on one side is the pure inventor; on the other side is the pure entrepreneur. For some, both sides of the scales are weighted heavily. These people are talented as both innovators and businesspeople.

EXAMPLE: William Lear, with his friend Elmer Wavering, co-invented the first car radio in 1930. Creating a radio that was audible in a moving vehicle was difficult enough, but exploiting that invention in the belt-tightening 1930s was more challenging. Lear proved as innovative at exploiting his invention as he was at creating it. Unable to afford a booth fee to show the product at an automotive trade show, Lear and Wavering parked outside the convention center, played their radio, and took orders in the parking lot. Lear's company sold the radio device under the trademark Motorola—combining "motor" and Victrola—and it was an instant hit. Had he not possessed a strong entrepreneurial streak, Lear's patented device might have been another footnote in automotive history. Instead, Motorola became an American institution.

But for Lear that was only the beginning. He went on to invent and exploit the 8-track tape format and navigation aids for aircraft. He later founded Lear, Inc., the supplier of the Lear Jet.

Clearly, not all inventors possess a strong entrepreneurial streak. For many, selling, marketing, and promoting their invention is less important than the pure act of innovation. Satisfaction is derived from the process, from spending time in the lab or workshop, and from the satisfaction of achieving a goal. If money accompanies the praise and acknowledgment, that's great, but for the pure inventor, it's not the main objective. For example, if you have ever received a patent, you will have also received a solicitation in the mail to purchase a fancy plaque replica of your patent. The fact that the patent plaque market is thriving suggests that the psychological rewards of inventing are very real and satisfying to many inventors. These truly pure inventors create mainly for the pleasure of creating.

There's nothing wrong with *not* wanting to delve deeply into business. We don't all aim to create a thriving company and spend our lives managing it. Many of us are content to create or invent and hope to turn over to someone else the more routine aspects of converting our "babies" into products or services. In fact, true idea creators and inventors typically lack the burning ambition of the more business-oriented person. It may be a low tolerance for business that propels you to invent devices to make our lives easier, safer, and more fun.

The Inventor-for-Royalties

Licensing is often preferable for those inventors who want to make money but care primarily about innovating and spending time in their lab. A license is simply an agreement in which you let someone else commercially use or develop your invention for a period of time. In return, you receive money— either a one-time payment or continuing payments called royalties. Your power to make this kind of agreement is based on the premise that you control the patent (or other legal rights) to your invention. Think of a license as giving a company permission to use your patent. As owner of the invention, you will always be the "licensor," and the party receiving the license for your invention is called the "licensee." What makes a license appealing—assuming it is the "right" license—is that the licensee assumes all of the business risks, from manufacturing to marketing to stopping those who infringe on the product's patents.

The licensing inventor sits by the mailbox and waits for the quarterly royalty checks.

Unlike a license, an assignment is a permanent transfer of ownership rights. When you assign your invention, you are the assignor and whoever purchases the rights is the assignee. An assignment is like the sale of a house, after which the seller no longer has any rights over the property. As the assignor, you may receive a lump sum payment or periodic royalty payments. Even though they have different legal meanings, the terms assignment and license are sometimes used interchangeably. Indeed, these two types of agreements sometimes seem to have the exact same effect. This is true in the case of an unlimited exclusive license, in which a licensee obtains the sole right to market the invention for an unlimited period of time. For this reason, you or your attorney must examine the specific conditions and obligations of each agreement rather than simply to rely on terms such as assignment and license.

You should also know the odds before you proceed into licensing. A study by Ed Zimmer and Ron Westrum revealed that about 13 percent of inventors who attempted to license their invention were successful. That's about one in eight. No doubt the other seven inventors were convinced that their invention would make money. (Note: This data is based on the persons who responded,

which probably skews the percentage positively. Those who were unsuccessful were probably less likely to respond at all.)

 For a thorough explanation of the invention licensing process, read *License Your Invention: Sell Your Idea & Protect Your Rights With a Solid Contract*, by Richard Stim (Nolo).

The Entrepreneurial Inventor

For those who place considerable weight on the entrepreneurial side of the scales, the financial reward of a license or assignment may seem unappealing— royalties often ranging from 2% to 10% of the net revenues. An entrepreneur may think, "Why should I give up my control and take a slice of the pie when I could keep the whole thing?" For this reason, inventors with a strong entrepreneurial drive often choose to form a business and to manufacture and market the product, a course of action that requires considerably more financial assistance than licensing.

Also, keep in mind that the same study by Zimmer and Westrum cited in the previous section revealed that close to half of the inventors who decided to take control of producing and marketing their invention claimed to be successful. That may be because the inventor with a strong entrepreneurial drive is usually

The Big Mac as a Paradigm

Maurice and Richard McDonald were brilliant innovators. Raymond Kroc was an entrepreneurial genius. Together they changed the American landscape. Examining this union of inventor and entrepreneur may help you understand and evaluate your own inventor personality.

In the early 1950s, the McDonald brothers, using their San Bernadino hamburger stand as a laboratory, invented most of the key methods and processes that became the foundation of the modern fast food industry. Their restaurant's walls were made of glass and featured two easily identifiable golden arches visible from the highway. The prices were low (fifteen-cent burgers and ten-cent fries), hamburgers were produced on an assembly line, the staff wore white uniforms, the restaurant was spotless, and the operation functioned like a manufacturing plant—uniform products produced efficiently at low cost. The brothers offered only nine-items—basically burgers, French fries, shakes, and pies—and eliminated glass and china (using paper plates and plastic utensils instead). Kroc later described it as "the most amazing merchandising operation I'd ever seen."

Kroc was a middle-aged salesman when he stumbled on the McDonald's restaurant in 1954, but he believed their methods were key to a phenomenal future. When he suggested that the brothers set up a business to market their innovations, the brothers demurred. They had tried expanding without luck and were happy to live off their profitable San Bernadino enterprise.

Kroc then proposed a licensing arrangement. In return for his right to use the name and innovations, the brothers would receive a royalty—a percentage of corporate profits. (The brothers later transferred all rights to Kroc's company for $2.7 million.)

In 1955, Kroc opened his first franchise outside Chicago and began a series of entrepreneurial innovations that were to change the course of the restaurant industry. He established size and shape specifications for food items and implemented quality control rules that added uniformity for customers of the chain. He also instituted a landmark training and research program—Hamburger University—that became the source for more innovations as well as a model for other corporations.

But Kroc's most brilliant innovation—indeed, the idea that turned McDonald's from a near-bankrupt chain to one of the largest businesses in the world—was for McDonald's to buy the land on which the chain's franchises operated, thus becoming the landlord for every franchisee.

The Big Mac as a Paradigm (continued)

This real estate strategy, combined with a public stock offering and massive national and international advertising campaigns, turned McDonald's into a global phenomenon.

In retrospect, both the McDonald Brothers and Kroc profited from their decisions. The brothers earned millions simply by licensing (and then selling) their innovations. As Kroc worked hard to turn the idea into a success, they sat back waiting for royalty checks. Kroc, however, amassed a much greater fortune—almost half a billion dollars—and created a global empire in the process. Kroc's obsession may have taken more of a personal toll—for example, the workaholic lifestyle that he instituted in his mid-fifties led to the end of his 39-year marriage in 1961.

---

obsessed with growing the business and thrives on the challenges—for example, how to manufacture your invention efficiently, how to acquire distribution, how to market to target audiences, how to eke out a profit from retail sales, how to collect from deadbeats, or how to enforce rights against infringers. Obviously, there are potentially much greater financial rewards than can be obtained from licensing, but the price that is paid personally and financially can be disastrous.

Charting Your Course

Your success in gaining finance depends on your intellectual honesty in analyzing your inventor personality. This is not a trivial concept. Keep in mind that even if you determine that you are a pure inventor, some degree of enterprise is still required. I don't mean that you will turn into a drudge. But the old quote attributed to Ralph Waldo Emerson about the public beating a path to your door if you invent a better mousetrap is utter nonsense. Emerson was a great philosopher, but as far as we know he never invented anything that made it to the market. You, alone, must beat the path—the path between you and the money you need.

Which is right for you? In terms of our goal—financing your invention—licensing usually requires much less capital than the alternative of manufacturing and marketing your invention yourself. In the case of licensing, what's usually required is money to patent your invention, create a prototype (or other suitable presentation to potential licensees), develop marketing materials, and, perhaps, solicit and negotiate with potential licensees. On the positive side, a successful licensing deal will free up an inventor to pursue inventing while still profiting from the last great idea. On the negative side, a bad licensing deal may tie up an innovation or, worse, result in legal battles over royalties.

You will usually need far more financing if you start your own business and manufacture and market your invention. Money is required for producing a prototype, creating tooling, or molds; mass producing the product; finding distribution; collecting payments, and to enforcing patent rights. On the positive side, the rewards are potentially much greater—which is precisely why it appeals to more entrepreneurial inventors. On the negative side, manufacturing and marketing are incredibly risky and can cause tremendous anxiety and engulf your personal life.

Unsure if you have a strong entrepreneurial drive? Honestly answer the following questions:

- **Are you a gifted salesperson?** An entrepreneur must sell, sell, and sell to every person in the food chain, whether it is an investor, banker, distributor, or customer. Consider Ron Popeil as an example. His success as a salesperson launched many inventions including the Veg-O-Matic, Pocket Fisherman, Mr. Microphone, the Buttoneer, Food Dehydrator, and, of course, the GLH Formula 9 Hair System (also known as Hair-in-a-Can). Regardless of the quality or intellectual value of his innovations, Popeil embodies the key to the successful entrepreneur and unstoppable skill at selling. If you lack this skill, you're probably not suited for entrepreneurial endeavors.

- **Are you a talented manager?** An entrepreneur must juggle many hats, and all of them require management skills. Consider the inventor of an ergonomic computer mouse who must travel abroad each year to supervise the manufacture of his device in a foreign factory as well as work with various international distributors and resellers. In his "free" time, he must work with the designers of his advertising and websites. If you can't delegate tasks well, don't get along with coworkers, or find it hard to organize your desk or keep track of complex tasks, do yourself a favor and avoid marketing and manufacturing.

- **Are you a business innovator?** You can't really call yourself a true entrepreneur unless your product or service involves innovation. Peter Drucker, America's foremost business sage, wrote in *Innovation and Entrepreneurship*, "Innovation is the specific tool of entrepreneurship, the means by which they exploit change as an opportunity for a different business or service." For example, say what you might about

Ron Popeil, he perfected an innovation—the infomercial—that changed the way products are sold on television. If you can only invent in the lab or workshop and not in the business world, then you may lack entrepreneurial skills and be better suited for licensing.

- **Are you a risk taker?** Some of us like to bungee jump from the Golden Gate Bridge and some of us don't. Entrepreneurs are willing to risk the whole pot on one hand. Every entrepreneur, whether it's Donald Trump, Richard Branson, Ron Popeil, or Ray Kroc, is willing to face down creditors or bankruptcy for a chance to come back for another round. If you're not a risk taker, then pursuing manufacturing and marketing is a poor decision.

In short, if business is your real game and creating an invention is just your means of acquiring something to sell, or if you live for the deal, you're not afraid of risks, you love to innovate in commerce, and you have the discipline to fight for market share, then marketing and manufacturing might be the right choice for you. If not, licensing would be the correct course.

■

Chapter 3

Six Tasks to Convert Your Idea Into a Product

Just as a plot is not a novel, an idea for an invention is not an invention. Until you can communicate the details of how your idea works by showing it in sketches and written specifications and instructions, all you have is a great idea. And ideas—adjusted for inflation—are a dollar a dozen nowadays.

I frequently receive calls from would-be inventors who have a great idea, one that they believe will make them and their supporters a fortune. These inventors honestly believe that the traditional sources of money should be willing to finance their great idea on the strength of its promise alone—even that investors should seek them out.

Folks, it just doesn't happen that way. Ideas are abundant. A highly creative person will have a couple of good ones before he or she finishes breakfast. And because ideas are all around us in abundance, the practical people who have made enough money to finance them are not likely to gravitate to your idea unless you take certain steps to develop it and demonstrate that it is not just another "me, too" concept. You need to show that your brainstorm has the potential to generate extraordinary profit. In short, you must take your great idea beyond its "Eureka!" phase. Just as a chemical process begins with natural material and is processed into a plastic, your idea must, as much as possible, evolve toward its predictable end. Its predictable end is the point at which the device is most attractive to consumers and investors.

EXAMPLE: Many people had the "itch" to create a device that could eliminate the tedious, labor-intensive work of hand sewing. But, obviously, it's difficult to attract investment with just an "idea" for a sewing machine. Elias Howe patented his "lockstitch" sewing machine in 1846. His device operated as follows: (1) a needle with an eye at the point (2) pushed through the cloth (3) creating a loop on the other side and (4) a shuttle on a track is then slipped a second thread through the loop, (5) creating what is called the lockstitch. But even with a precise definition, a prototype, and sufficient investment, Howe was unable to successfully market his invention. In other words, even though his machine was innovative, it did not take the sewing machine to its predictable end as a marketable invention. That was accomplished by Isaac Singer, who built the first commercially successful sewing machine. In Singer's machine, the needle moved up and down (rather than side to side) *and* was powered by a foot treadle. The treadle, rather than a hand crank, proved to be the innovative tipping point that made the sewing machine a commercial success.

Ironically, Howe, like many patent holders, earned his fortune by suing Singer (not from marketing his own invention). Howe claimed that Singer's machine infringed his patent and won a sizeable portion of the Singer royalties—an award that, in retrospect, seems unjustified. Twelve years before Howe (1834), Elias Hunt had invented the same device as Howe but had abandoned his patent because of a concern that his invention would cause massive unemployment. We'll see that under modern definitions of "prior art," it's likely that Howe would not be able to achieve the same results today in a patent lawsuit.

As the invention of the sewing machine demonstrates, even if you have worked out all of the details and can show on paper how your invention works, this is barely adequate to explain or demonstrate your invention. Nor is it a viable means of measuring its success. Your invention often doesn't fully evolve until you create a prototype or working model of your invention, a development that is a much more effective way to evoke enthusiastic response and enlist support. And, as in the case of the sewing machine, the most important evolution may come as a result of a final tweak or brainstorm.

In this chapter, I'll explain how to define, develop, protect, and perfect your idea. Unless you take these essential steps, you will have a difficult, if not impossible, job acquiring funding. Once you've completed these tasks you will be better prepared, and your great idea will be more presentable when you seek financing. This chapter discusses six tasks you must accomplish before approaching investors.

The six steps required to define, develop, protect, and perfect your invention are understood among experienced inventors but are seldom generally understood by first-time inventors. You should be prepared to come up with self-financing for most or all of the tasks described.

- **Define your invention in writing and drawings.** An adequate written and visual explanation is the bottom-line requirement for seeking money. Expense: $0.

- **Assess marketability.** It's not enough to believe your invention will make money; you must objectively assess its chances in the marketplace using established criteria. Expense: Expect to pay $300 or less.

- **Determine if your invention is patentable**. If your invention is not novel or does not otherwise meet the standards of patent protection, you will have a difficult (if not impossible) time obtaining money. Expense: Expect to pay between $500 and $1,000 for a simple invention.

- **Make a prototype.** The capability to demonstrate your invention may be the key to funding success. Expense: Expect to pay between $300 and $3,000 depending on the complexity of your invention.

The Shower Master™: Converting an Idea to Product

Anthony Ruggiero observed water damage in several rental units he owned. Tenants had shower mishaps that affected bathroom floors and the ceilings of the units below. Anthony observed similar damage in motels and hotels. His conclusion: Shower curtains don't seal against the end-walls of the showers.

Ruggiero reasoned that if he had a shower curtain that wrapped in at each end, such damage would be prevented. When he attempted to design such a unit, he found that wall mountings—the simplest means of accomplishing his goal—wouldn't work because they required drilling, often through ceramic tile.

Anthony ultimately perfected and defined his invention, Shower Master™, a device that slides flawlessly on the user's existing bar and installs without tools. (See Fig. 1, below.). To achieve this, Ruggiero used a curved sliding end-track piece for the inner curtain (the liner). This piece fixes the liner in its curved position and yet slides on the bar. A small counter-weight keeps the liner from sagging due to its own weight.

Ruggiero did typical market research: talking with potential customers and pursuing market channels. He determined the need for his product by his first-hand knowledge of damage in most of his own rental units and observation of damage in motels and hotels. He also talked with numerous homeowners and rental property managers. Approximately two-thirds reported water damage from careless shower users. The interviewees were interested in a way to avoid this type of damage. Based on his initial research, Ruggiero patented his invention and then financed injection-molded production tooling. The cost in the U.S. would have been $170,000. Ruggiero paid about half of that in Taiwan.

Ruggiero submitted designs to several specialized producers of plumbing products such as Better Bath and Zenith Bath Products, hoping to license his invention. He also submitted it to a catalog agent and worked with a marketing agent. As this book was going to press, Ruggiero had been offered a potential licensing deal.

SHOWER MASTER™ Spray Control System
"Curves Your Curtain Liner To Keep Shower Spray Inside The Bathtub"

INSTALLS IN MINUTES
*
NO TOOLS REQUIRED
*
PARTS SNAP TOGETHER FOR EASY ASSEMBLY
*
SIMPLY PLACE ONTO SHOWER ROD
*
INCLUDES WANDS TO PREVENT TORN CURTAINS
*
OPENS AND CLOSES SMOOTHLY ON ROLLERS
*
USES STANDARD 70" SHOWER CURTAINS & LINERS (NOT INCLUDED)
*
MATCHING CURTAIN RINGS INCLUDED

Crafted With Pride in the USA

SANITARY
*
KEEPS BATHROOM FLOOR AND WALLS DRY
*
STOPS AFTER SHOWER MOP-UPS
*
PREVENTS COSTLY WATER DAMAGE
*
HELPS PREVENT HARMFUL MOLDS
*
EASY REMOVAL AND REPLACEMENT OF CURTAIN LINERS
*
WON'T RUST OR CORRODE
*
PROTECTS LEFT AND RIGHT SIDES

Only One Side Illustrated (Contents include left & right units)
* Shower Curtain, Liner, Shower Rod & Showerhead not included

CAN ADD AN EXCITING NEW LOOK TO YOUR BATHROOM

ATTENTION: Product may not be suitable for use with some spring loaded (tension) shower rods. Product functions best when used with a permanent, securely installed standard 1" diameter metal shower rod.

- **Patent it (if possible).** Acquiring a patent (or assuring a lender that an application has been filed) is often crucial when seeking money. Expense: Getting a patent can cost between $5,000 and $10,000.
- **Test market it.** Having real people test a real version of your invention may provide information that is essential to lending decisions. Expense: Can cost several hundred to several thousand dollars.

These six steps represent my crash course in the development, protection, and marketing of a great idea and invention. A crash course, that's all. Each of these steps justifies a book (and there are several good books available—see Chapter 12 for recommendations).

These six steps may be compressed or may overlap, or you may find that one or two are not needed. Below is a real-world example of how one inventor progressed.

You can create a simple spreadsheet to estimate your expenses. A sample is provided below. If possible, try to spread the expenses over the expected time period—that is, all of these expenses won't occur at the same time.

Once you know your expected costs, you'll be better prepared to analyze which of your sources of financing is best suited for each expense.

Define Your Invention

A professor of mine once said, "If you can't write it, you don't know it." That seemed harsh. A monkey certainly knows a banana, but it can't write a definition. I think that what my professor was getting at was the level of sophistication that we experience in communicating complex ideas.

When you invent something, you are doing more than experiencing the "itch" of innovation; you are defining a way to satisfy the itch, and you must be able to convey that exact definition to others. The very act of writing a definition of what you have invented, and sketching

Task	Mar	Apr	May	Jun	Jul	Aug	Sep	Oct	Nov	Dec	Total
Marketability Study	$300										$300
Patent Search			$1,000								$1,000
Prototype					$3,000						$3,000
Patent Filing							$7,500				$7,500
Test Market										$8,500	$8,500
Total for Year											$20,300

or drawing it, forces you to invent rather than just have a great idea.

The detailed definition of your invention on paper has three important early uses:

- **It establishes the date of invention.** Under U.S. patent law, the first to invent (not the first to file, as in other countries) acquires patent rights. Determining who first invented something is based upon written documentation, in the form either of journal records, patent filings, or other documented evidence.
- **It can aid in assessing marketability.** In the early stages of idea development, a clearly written description can help you determine if your idea has commercial potential.
- **It can assist in assessing patentability.** A clearly written description of your invention is essential for searching patent records and other prior art to determine whether your invention qualifies for a patent.

A few years ago I received a call from a woman who wanted me to develop a new kind of kitchen mop—one that had a fluid reservoir and a disposable pad. I declined the job because I was too involved in other projects to be able to devote the time that would have been required. Not long afterward, Clorox came out with the disposable-pad mop that feeds a cleaning fluid by way of trigger action. Now, if that woman had defined her invention exhaustively, and it had had the features of the Clorox mop, and she had begun the patent process with, let's say, a provisional patent application (see "The Provisional Patent Application," below) even a few days before Clorox filed its application, she may have been able to get some kind of monetary settlement from Clorox, even without going to court. Keep in mind that that the timely coincidence of great ideas is neither accidental nor rare, and the only way to sort out such disputes is through written documentation.

EXAMPLE: Perhaps the most famous case of coincidental inventing is that of Elisha Gray and Alexander Graham Bell, who submitted papers covering the invention of the telephone to the patent office on the same day, within hours of each other! In truth, this rush to the patent office wasn't that much of a coincidence. Elisha Gray and Alexander Graham Bell didn't just get the idea for the telephone out of the blue one day. For years, telegraph operators had been interpreting the dots and dashes of the telegraph machine by the audible rhythm of the device, thus dispensing with the cumbersome and relatively slow paper strip. It occurred to a lot of inventive people that telegraphers were sending vibrations over wires, and sound was vibration, so the great idea was to figure out how to convert sound to electrical current.

Eventually, that breakthrough was made by vibrating a bunch of carbon granules with a diaphragm, and thereby varying the resistance to the current in the circuit. So, why did Bell become rich and famous, while Gray, who is hardly ever mentioned, did not? Because Bell's description of his invention in his patent application and his drawings of variable resistance means, diaphragms, and electromagnets clearly demonstrated how his invention would work. These were witnessed and dated. Gray's records, in comparison, were poor. After review by the Patent Office, the patent was awarded to Bell. Another reason Bell received the patent was that Gray never bothered to fight for it. Gray, a businessman, didn't believe that the telephone had any commercial potential and filed his patent documents as an afterthought. He and his business partners and attorneys believed that the telephone was a novelty not worth fighting over. Only later, after Western Union funded his attacks, did Gray mount a major (and unsuccessful) legal challenge against Bell's patent.

Like the telephone, every great invention is preceded by information, thought, and materials that have prepared the way for it. An ongoing evolution drives the next step, the next great idea, and the one after that, and if you don't come up with the next one, someone else will. This is always easy to see in retrospect, but not always obvious at the time of invention.

Maybe I've belabored this point, but I'm sure you will agree that if you have a great idea for an invention, you should document its development.

There are many ways to do this, the most common of which is a journal (preferably one with a sewn binding). The inventor makes timely entries regarding development and testing and has it witnessed by someone who will be credible to a judge and a jury (for example, someone who will not profit from it later on and who is not your spouse or your brother-in-law, and so on). You must record and have witnessed every step of major significance in converting your great idea to a perfected invention. Sketches, even crude ones, add to the effectiveness of your entries. Simple journals, often titled simply "Record," can be found in the bookkeeping section at Staples, Office Depot, and so forth. These books have sewn-in pages that are numbered. No one can accuse you of "creative" entries such as could be done if you kept your journal in a three-ring binder.

Another popular means of documenting and defining your invention is a provisional patent application (see "The Provisional Patent Application," below), a document that is sent to the USPTO and, for one year, preserves your date of invention.

The Provisional Patent Application

The provisional patent application offers an effective, fast, and cheap way to safeguard your place in line at the United States Patent and Trademark Office (USPTO) until you file a regular patent application. A provisional patent application consists of text and drawings that describe how to make and use your invention. It's a short document—often 5-10 pages—written in plain English, not the complex language commonly associated with regular patent applications. In fact, if you've written a technical article that accurately describes how to make and use your invention, you can submit that as part of your application. You do not need to hire a draftsperson to prepare formal drawings; you can furnish informal drawings as long as they—in conjunction with your written statement—show how to make and use your invention. As soon as you send the description, the drawings, and a cover sheet to the USPTO by Express Mail (along with the $100 fee), you establish an effective filing date for your invention, and you can use the term "patent pending" on your invention— for 12 months from the filing date. A provisional patent application will not, by itself, get you a patent. In order to patent your invention and obtain some of the benefits listed above, you must file a regular patent application—a more complex document—and the patent must be approved by the USPTO. The provisional patent application is a simple, inexpensive strategy to preserve your rights while you decide whether to file for a regular patent. But if you want a patent based on your provisional patent application filing date, you will have to file a regular application within a year after you file your provisional application.

For more information on filing a provisional patent application, read *Patent Pending in 24 Hours*, by Richard Stim and David Pressman (Nolo).

Assess Marketability

When you have defined your invention on paper—not only your great idea, but the mechanism or means by which you will accomplish it—you are ready to obtain an objective assessment of its marketability. Keep in mind that your friends and family and even most patent agents and attorneys feel that it is not their place to advise inventors on the market feasibility of the invention presented to them. This is especially true of attorneys. Suppose they discourage the inventor from proceeding, and another inventor succeeds with the very same invention. The attorney would be liable for a lawsuit, or at least a lot of bad-mouthing among local inventors. Thus, the origin of the well-quoted odds that 95 percent of patents never earn more than their cost.

Don't be discouraged with these grim statistics. They are based on the experience of inventors who don't read books, don't plan, and don't know how to get the money they need; not you. I'll guide you through the maze and help you to raise your odds well beyond the five percent success rate often quoted.

There are a small number of universities that evaluate inventions for inventors at a very reasonable price. My favorite is the WIN Innovation Institute (www .innovation-institute.com), affiliated with Southwest Missouri State University (SMSU). At the time of this writing their fee was $250. The Institute uses the Preliminary Innovation Evaluation Service (PIES) system of evaluation. This covers 42 separate points that determine how probable it is that your invention will be accepted in the marketplace.

In our zeal to drive our inventions forward, we often are unaware of many of these 42 points and spend wasted money on a patent. I see this much, if not most, of the time as I work with inventors.

There are three inventions that appear time and time again and seem to be unmarketable: a dental floss holder, a safe syringe, and a toilet seat lifter. In the past ten years I have had three clients come to me with dental floss holders and two with toilet seat holders and, although they are not clients, I am acquainted with two inventors of safe syringes—the kind that reposition the needle after the injection, and thereby protect the nurse or doctor from accidental viral or bacterial transfer.

Here, in my opinion, are the reasons why these inventions don't reach the market: Dental floss holders have been tried with generally poor consumer acceptance. There is one disposable holder that has merit, but, judging from the difficulty one has in finding it on the racks in drug stores, I assume that it isn't a popular seller. People don't like to floss no matter what the system. But fingers appear to win out as the most versatile holders of floss.

There are several patents on safe syringes, and one or two are actually in use. According to my friend and fellow inventor, Joe Blake (60 patents), the marketing channels are settled on a syringe that works. And, unless a novel design arises that has some extraordinary benefit, the entrenched products can't be displaced. The tooling is paid for, the customers are used to the model they now use, and there is no point in risking a new model even if it is less expensive or slightly better in some way.

Ah, the toilet-seat lifter. This item can't really be considered much of an invention. It is too obvious, and therefore probably won't pass the Patent Office requirement of "unobviousness" to someone skilled in the area (a toilet seat maker). And the fact that the consumer would have to install it with screws is a definite impediment to sales. But the main problem, as I see it, is marketing. A simple item like this probably won't sell well if priced beyond two or three dollars. Even a package of two at $4.95 wouldn't be attractive to most catalogers.

By obtaining a professional evaluation before spending any significant amount of money, you may find that your invention, even though it has considerable merit, isn't likely to succeed in the marketplace, and your options are to fight against the odds or to abandon your venture. I know that you don't even want to think about these two possibilities, but you must be realistic. Some inventions cannot succeed even though they have great merit and the world needs them. Here's another example.

EXAMPLE: I was given a free sample of a small plastic wedge set that could be used to level a four-legged table that rocks when you lean on it. Everyone experiences a rocking table in a restaurant now and then, and this device solves the problem neatly. Did the inventor have a crowd beating a path to his door to buy the product, which was ready for the market? No. Even though it offers true utility, there is simply no good way to market the product. It can't sell for more than a dollar or so. Thus, it can't be sold through catalogs, which typically can't make a profit on items priced at less than somewhere between $5 and $10, depending on the catalog. It can't be sold in retail stores, because its market is the food service business. And it won't make a good advertising or promotional giveaway, because no one will see it once it is installed.

Don't be certain that your great idea is going to make you a fortune! Get a second opinion from someone who isn't your mother or your spouse—or even a complete stranger, who, out of courtesy, will probably tell you what you hope to hear. The most easily financed inventions are the ones that we abandon before we spend a lot of money on them. I'm not being a killjoy here. I'm just saying that if your invention won't make it in the marketplace, then it is better to know that before spending a few thousand dollars on it. You'll need that money for your next great idea or invention.

You can also obtain valuable advice about your invention by soliciting advice from potential customers—preferably with a well-prepared questionnaire.

EXAMPLE: Kieu Phan invented the BraBall®, a plastic "clamshell" enclosure for washing, drying, and storing brassieres and bikini tops. This patented (U.S. Pat. 6,742,683) device preserves the bra's shape and contour by preventing bunching and denting, keeps underwires from piercing the fabric, and prevents straps from tangling and snagging on other items.

The BraBall proceeded through a typical invention evolution. The inventor first described the device in rough sketches. A prototyper made a thermal-formed prototype. The shape of the inner "cup-form" was initially deemed unsatisfactory.

A professional designer redefined the shape of the cup-form with measurements from a padded bra. A stereolithography prototype was made. Design changes were made to latch and hole shapes. A second stereolithography prototype was made. A trial determined that the cup-form bounced around during washing. The cup-form was redesigned to lock into the outer ball. A third stereolithography prototype was made. 3-D drawings were sent to two mold-makers for offshore quotes. After a study of production tooling, and incidental hardware, a pilot run was ordered. Minor changes were then requested, and production followed. Kieu Phan then carried on market research using focus groups and her own extensive surveys using questionnaires in malls.

The questionnaire, below, provides a good example of do-it-yourself marketing research.

Survey for BraBall®

Check *all* answers that apply to you.

☐ Yes ☐ No   1. Would you purchase the BraBall for yourself?

If yes, why? _____

_____

☐ a. to protect the longevity of my bras

☐ b. to save money

☐ c. to save time and energy from hand washing my bras

☐ Yes ☐ No   2. Would you purchase the BraBall for someone else?

☐ Yes ☐ No   3. Do you think the BraBall is too big?

☐ Yes ☐ No   4. Do you think it is durable (able to last a long time)?

If no, why not? _____

_____

☐ Yes ☐ No   5. Do you think it might damage your washing machine?

If yes, why? _____

_____

☐ Yes ☐ No   6. Do you think it might damage you clothes?

If yes, why? _____

7. What specific changes or improvements would you make to the BraBall? _____

_____

8. What would you consider to be a reasonable price for the BraBall? _____

9. What price would be so low that YOU would question the quality of the BraBall? _____

10. What is the maximum price you would consider paying for a BraBall? _____

11. What do you feel might be the biggest obstacle, if any, to your purchasing the BraBall?

☐ price   ☐ skepticism   ☐ need

☐ other_____

12. Where would you want to buy a BraBall? (Please check all answers that apply)

☐ a. department store (Foley's, Dillard's, J.C. Penny, etc.)

☐ b. lingerie store (Victoria's Secret)

☐ c. grocery store (H.E.B., Albertson's, Randall's)

☐ d. QVC and HSN

☐ e. catalogs

☐ f. TV infomercial

☐ g. on the Internet

☐ h. large retail store (Linens 'N Things, Container Store, Bed Bath & Beyond, etc.)

☐ i. mega retail store (Wal-Mart,. K-Mart, Target, etc.)

13. In what specific store(s) would you want to see the BraBall offered? _____

_____

_____

_____

_____

14. What motivates you to buy new bras?

☐ a. Bras get old.

☐ b. Bras get damaged (straps loses elasticity, padding bunches, underwires bend and fabric snags)

☐ c. Bras get discolored.

☐ d. I like to buy new bras.

15. How much do you usually pay for a bra? _____

16. How often do you buy bras?
    - ☐ a. at least once a month or more
    - ☐ b. at least once every six months
    - ☐ c. at least once a year
    - ☐ d. every 2-5 years

17. When you buy bras, how many do you typically purchase at one time? _____

☐ Yes ☐ No 18. Do you wear padded bras?

If yes, how padded? ☐ slightly padded

☐ heavily padded

What kind of padding?

☐ air   ☐ gel   ☐ foam

☐ silicone   ☐ water mix   ☐ don't know

19. What's your bra cup size?

☐ A   ☐ B   ☐ C   ☐ D and up

☐ Yes ☐ No 20. Do you wash your bras in the washer?

If yes, are you satisfied with how they come out?

☐ Yes ☐ No

If no, why not? _____

☐ Yes ☐ No 21. Do you do anything special in order to wash your bra?

If yes, what? _____

22. What is your age?

☐ 13-18   ☐ 19-24   ☐ 25-34   ☐ 35-44

☐ 45-54   ☐ 55-65   ☐ 65 or over

Measuring Marketability and Extraordinary Profits

Those who may finance or license your invention sometimes start their examination of marketability by asking, "Are there customers who will perceive the invention as something more valuable than that which now serves their need or want or solves their problem?" This is a different question from, "Is this a brilliant invention?" Investors know that brilliant inventions without an equally brilliant demand can be a dud.

Sometimes, a graph is used to measure marketability, as shown below.

```
                new technology
                      │
    • a               │            b •
                      │
                      │
  existing market     │        new market
──────────────────────┼──────────────────────
                      │
                      │
                      │
                      │
                existing technology
```

Your invention is represented by the dot.

Dot "b" would seem ideal—a new technology and a new market. And for some entrepreneurs it is ideal. The Apple computer, which was angel financed at the start, was a new technology in a new market. Millions of dollars of venture capital are required to create an invention in this position, and millions more to create its market. Even if all of the costs of developing the invention into a product are paid at this point, the costs of creating the market are almost certainly too high to attract an investor.

Dot "a" on the graph scores a home run. The difficulties, uncertainties, and enormous expense of creating a market are not present. And a new technology is available to service the existing market. Assuming the new technology can be manufactured at a cost that will accommodate a selling price that the customer perceives as acceptable, it has the potential for extra-ordinary profit.

A dot in the lower-right quadrant could mean new profits if your invention is patented and you have some kind of edge in the new market. In such case, your invention may be the discovery or creation of the new market rather than the means of satisfying that market.

A dot in the lower-left quadrant will probably strike out. Your invention is a "me, too."

Now, if you find that the placement of your invention on the graph does not suggest that you have a winner—an innovative product that will service an already existing market—you should rethink your situation. You probably won't excite any investors (except friends and relatives) to the point of investing. If that's the case, do you really want to risk failure? You might succeed, but you are "sweeping water up hill," as my old boss, Neil Blair, would say. Your strategy in this case is to save the money you would spend on developing and protecting your invention, and go on to a new invention or great idea that drops in high and wide in the upper-left quadrant on our graph.

You will find a few independent evaluators advertised in *Inventors' Digest*. Although legitimate, these evaluators may have something more to sell you than an evaluation. They may want to do a market survey, for example, and the price may be a few thousand dollars. You will have to decide whether such service is of more value to you than the WIN Innovation Institute-type evaluation. If you have the money at the outset, a market survey could support your quest for invested money, especially if you intend to produce and market your invention. But be cautious, as always.

Watch Out for Scam Marketing Companies

Watch out for scam artists who prey on inventors. Inventor frauds, including bogus promises to perform market assessments or to file patents are commonplace. The USPTO website (www.uspto.gov) and the Federal Trade Commission website (www.ftc.gov) both offer advice on how to avoid disreputable invention promotion companies.

Below are some tips that may help you in identifying a scam marketer.

Invention marketing companies prey on inventors and innovators. Inventors pay anywhere from $1,500 to $10,000 and (despite the promises) are left with no protection and no prospects. When inventors complain or attempt to sue under the contract, they rarely collect damages even if they win their lawsuit. The annual profits for these marketing companies is estimated to be in the millions.

Most invention marketing scams operate in the same manner. They combine unrealistic promises with high pressure sales techniques. They offer to evaluate your product, yet they never criticize or reject any products they consider. Some common methods employed by these firms include:

- Advertising through television, radio, and classified ads in newspapers and magazines.
- Offering free information to help patent and market inventions.
- Advertising a toll-free "800" number that inventors can call for written information (usually brochures about the promoters).
- Sales calls asking for information about yourself, your ideas, and a sketch of the invention.
- Offering to do a free preliminary review of your invention.
- Suggesting a market evaluation on your idea and charging anywhere

from several hundred to several thousand dollars.

- Supplying a marketing evaluation report that makes vague and general statements that could apply to any invention, not just yours ("You could make $2-3 million dollars from your sprocket mirror invention."). The report provides no hard evidence that there is a consumer market for your invention.

- Asking the inventor to pay a fee plus a percentage of future royalties. The "future royalties" portion of the payment is part of the scam, because the inventor is lead to believe that the invention has commercial value when no actual research has been done to support this claim.

- Seeking more money after the preliminary evaluation (from $2,000 to $8,000) to acquire adequate legal protection for your invention. Despite the promises of "government protection," the company merely files a Document Disclosure form or a Provisional Patent Application. Because the paperwork resulting from these efforts has U.S. Government letterhead and looks similar to a patent, inventors mistakenly believe they have obtained patent protection. Sometimes the company may file a design patent, which will only protect the appearance of your invention, not its functions. In other

words, the companies create a false sense of security and belief that the company is earning its fees.

- Seeking more money to promote your invention. The scam marketer informs you that more money is necessary to take your product to the "right" companies. Instead of actually presenting your product, the marketer sends you a list of companies, most (or all) of which will have no relation to your invention.

- Confusing the issue. The scam marketer may offer two choices for a share of royalties—for example, a 15% royalty if the inventor pays $12,000 or a 20% royalty if the inventor pays $20,000. This "sucker psychology" distracts the inventor from the more obvious fact that the inventor will end with zero dollars.

Keep in mind that the evaluations performed by legitimate companies usually cost several hundred dollars and result in a critique that is particular to your invention and the appropriate industry.

Although scam marketers may seek a percentage of profits, they actually make their money by exorbitant upfront fees that are unrelated to any service that they perform. As a general rule, a person or company that demands more than $1,000 in upfront fees and will not furnish you with a list of clients is probably a scam marketing venture. If you are in doubt, some of the following methods of checking on a marketing company are recommended:

- Ask for a written estimate of the total cost of services (if they are a scam they will hesitate or be unwilling to provide a firm estimate).
- Ask what specific standards are used to evaluate your commercial success.
- Ask for a disclosure of the company's success and rejection rates. Success rates show the number of clients who make more money from their invention than they paid the firm. Rejection rates reflect the percentage of all ideas or inventions that were found unacceptable by the invention promotion company. As a general rule, a reputable marketing firm rejects most of the inventions.
- Ask for a list of satisfied clients.
- Investigate the company before making any commitments.

You may feel comfortable dealing with an invention marketing firm because the contract you sign provides for "refunds" or has a "money-back guarantee," or perhaps you believe that you can always sue the company in your local small claims court. Good luck! Remember that these companies did not get where they are by furnishing refunds. Regardless of the contract that you sign, the practical reality is that once a dishonest company has your money, you will never get it back. When in doubt, don't send money.

Assess Patentability

Suppose that you received a high score on your marketability assessment. Now what? Well, if you plan on licensing (what I describe as an inventor-for-royalties), you will probably have to obtain a patent. The philosophy of most corporations is that you, the inventor, must prove that your invention is novel by patenting it or, in less common cases, protecting it by some other form of intellectual property such as copyright, trademark, trade secret, or design patent. Without this proprietary protection, the corporation will often consider it in the public domain and will feel free to use it even though its personnel hadn't thought of it before you submitted it. As a general rule, no company will pay you royalties on an invention that is not patented. (There are a few rare exceptions, such as the toy industry, that license unpatented inventions proposed to them because, by the time the patent issues, the toy is likely to be obsolete.)

Probably the most important hurdle to patentability is whether your invention is novel. An invention is novel if it differs from previous inventions or existing knowledge. To determine if your invention is novel you must search "prior art," which is any form of published information that describes an invention like yours. (See "What Is Prior Art?," below.) Most often, prior art is thought of as patents, and most patent searches consist only of looking at issued patents. But a magazine or newspaper article that describes your invention will, if discovered by the patent examiner, bar you from getting a patent. And, if not discovered, such article could be used to "break" your patent after it is issued.

Another good reason to search for prior art: to avoid claims of patent infringement. Searching prior art does not only turn up ideas and inventions that might prevent you from getting a patent; it can also alert you to a potential disaster. If someone holds an in-force patent for an invention that claims to do the same thing as your invention, your manufacture, use, sale, or offer for sale of the same invention would infringe this patent. And, if you sell your invention knowing someone else has a patent, you may be liable for increased financial damages.

I strongly recommend having a patent attorney or patent agent search the patent files and prepare a patentability opinion. A search without a professional evaluation and written patentability opinion is not worth much. It is sort of like dumping a jigsaw puzzle out on a table. All of the pieces may be there, but until someone sorts them out, compares them with other pieces into which they fit, and assembles them into a picture, you don't really know what you have. Patent claims, which are the essence of every patent, are like the pieces of the

puzzle: Each claim from a competing patent found in the search hopefully only fits along side the claims you hope to have accepted. If a competing claim is found to overlap one of your claims, the examiner will reject that claim. If all of your anticipated claims are identical to competing claims, your entire patent application will be denied. Thus, patentability is best determined by a professional unless you are very experienced in the business of claims interpretation.

You can do your own preliminary patent search conveniently on the Internet, and several books such as *Patent It Yourself* and *Patent Pending in 24 Hours* (both from Nolo) explain how to perform an Internet search. This can even be done for free at the USPTO website (www.uspto.gov). This type of search (known as a "knockout search") may unearth prior art that convinces you that your idea is not novel. For this reason, a knockout search is an inexpensive way to see if easily identified patents will knock out your chances for a patent. For a list of fee-based patent databases that include more than the USPTO—for example, foreign patents and other prior art—see the resources in Chapter 12.

If a search that you, yourself, have done on the Internet reveals a patent on an invention that is exactly like yours, you know then that you probably will not be able to obtain a patent. Be careful here, too, because a description and

What Is Prior Art?

In order to qualify for a patent, your invention must differ from previous inventions or existing knowledge. The USPTO refers to existing inventions and knowledge as prior art. If your invention differs physically in some way from the prior art, you have made it over this primary hurdle (but not necessarily all of the hurdles to patentability). Prior art includes:

- anything in public use or on sale in the U.S. more than one year before the filing date of your patent application
- anything that was publicly known or used or made or built in this country by another person before your date of invention
- prior patents issued, or prior publications dated more than one year before the filing date of the patent or any time before the date of invention, or
- U.S. patents that have a filing date prior to your date of invention. The effective date of a patent that is based on a provisional patent application is the date the provisional is filed.

a drawing may appear to be exactly like your invention, but a professional reading of the claims section of the patent may reveal that your invention is significantly different.

Professional patent searchers examine more than just the obvious class and subclass for your invention and will almost always find more pertinent patents than you will find with an Internet search. The most convenient way to get a patent search is to have your patent agent or patent attorney arrange it for you.

This will cost more than if you hire a searcher, but the agent or attorney is bound to feel comfortable with his "own guy." If you bring the results of a search that you have arranged for on your own to your agent or attorney and later, after filing the patent application, the patent examiner comes back with a patent for an invention that is identical to yours, your agent or attorney will not feel any responsibility for having missed this key patent.

A patent search alone doesn't mean much until you or your agent or attorney analyzes the pertinent patents that were supplied by the searcher and provides a professional, written opinion on the chances of a quality patent being granted. According to the U.S. Patent and Trademark office (USPTO) statistics, only 65 percent of applications result in an issued patent. You will almost always find prior art in doing a patent search.

The question is, can you "write around" the prior art and still have a strong patent if and when you do?

On the other hand, if you find no other identical invention, this is not necessarily good news. As the scientist Carl Sagan once said, "Absence of evidence is not evidence of absence." A professional searcher knows how to search other patent categories that may be used by the patent examiner in the Patent Office to reject your application.

A patentability opinion is potentially self-serving for the agent or attorney, and you are at the mercy of his or her ethics. It is almost always possible to patent some trivial feature of your invention, but a weak patent will not be attractive to a prospective licensee, and you probably won't succeed in licensing it. So, if your agent or attorney advises you to file, take your time, and discuss which features of your invention he or she believes to be patentable and how strong the patent will be. Fortunately, most patent professionals are ethical and won't advise you to file unless they are fairly sure of getting you a worthwhile patent.

A patent search, as of this writing, costs around $250. And the search plus patentability opinion costs between $500 and $1,000, depending on the hourly rate of the agent or attorney and the complexity of your invention. For more information on patent searching resources, see Chapter 12.

Get a Prototype

It's not essential to create a prototype, but I strongly recommend it. A prototype or working model of your invention may enable your agent or attorney to get a stronger patent, because it can disclose refinements or even essential features that your written definition lacks. Not only is a prototype useful before filing a patent, it can also aid in your early financing and marketing attempts. However, I advise against spending money on a prototype unless your patentability opinion is favorable.

Whether you file your patent application first or make your prototype first is not always clear. Keep in mind that Alexander Graham Bell did not produce a working prototype of his telephone until after his patent had issued. If your invention is very simple but costs more to prototype than filing your patent application, it makes sense to file the application first, preserve your capital if it is scarce, and gain the advantage of the earlier filing date. Also, you can then use the "patent applied for" status as leverage in your quest for finance. If your invention is complex and still evolving, you may gain by making the prototype first so that your design is perfected, and your patent professional will have all of the features and how they relate as the basis for a complete specification and strong claims.

As with any expensive purchase, get price quotes from more than one prototyper to save capital and to find the best source. Find prototypers in the classified ads in *Inventors' Digest* or by using search terms such as "Prototypers" or "Model makers" in Internet search engines. Sometimes you can find them in local yellow page directories.

Still another source, especially if your invention involves electrical as well as mechanical attributes, may be your local university. Universities that have strong engineering departments often have prototyping facilities that are looking for business. Seasoned professionals supervise these facilities, and advanced students do much of the work. Because the universities are not-for-profit, you may get the best price as well as competence. Don't neglect to solicit pricing from other sources, however.

In making a prototype, inventors often discover features that are patentable. Sometimes these features seem too simple to form the basis for a strong patent. And sometimes they become the key to a strong patent. Like a grain of sand in one's shoe, a detail feature of your invention may be an irritant to a competitor—something that makes your invention significantly better than whatever now is being used to accomplish its same purpose.

Prototype prices will run from a few hundred dollars to several thousand. One of my clients was recently quoted $25,000 by a New York university for a relatively complicated invention

that involved a heating chamber and motorized platform. Another client who invented a key-assist device for persons with severe arthritis in their hands paid less than $400 for his prototype. Whatever the price, if it is fair, this is a "cost of entry": one of the costs to develop your invention so that you can license it or produce it.

Patent Your Invention

To patent or not to patent, that is the question. Experienced inventors—at least those who have made money from their inventions—look on the patent as a tool to hopefully ensure both their product's exclusivity and their continued profit or royalties. But, as important as patent may be, rushing to get a patent before you've perfected your invention can be a waste of time and money. Many uninitiated inventors make the mistake of running to a patent attorney as a first step, or at least a very early step, in their venture. These inventors view the patent as a kind of credential or validation of their worth as an inventor, rather than as a means of monopolizing a specific technology.

All patents are *not* equal. A poorly drafted patent, a patent that does not reflect your recent innovations, or a patent that is too narrow will not allow you to monopolize your invention. And, for that reason, you will be unable to attract investors, because your claim for proprietary rights is so limited as to be ineffective. That's why it's essential, prior to seeking a patent, for you to carefully assess your invention's marketability and patentability. It's also why you may need to consult a patent professional (a patent lawyer or patent agent) to write or review—in case you write your own—a patent application.

Filing and acquiring a patent is a lengthy process—all the more reason why you should do it at the right time and get it right when you do it. You may also choose to delay the process (or bypass it entirely) with one of the patent alternatives listed below.

You *Can* Write It Yourself

Numerous inventors have obtained patents on their own—many using the method attorney David Pressman explains in detail in his popular book, *Patent It Yourself* (Nolo). Pressman is a patent attorney, and his book is the classic in this field. It is so good that patent agents and attorneys often keep a copy out of sight in a desk drawer. Even if you don't write one word of your own application, I urge you to obtain *Patent It Yourself* and study it. This book is a marvelous, down-to-earth instruction in the art of the patent and will save its cost many times over by educating you about how to work effectively with your agent or attorney.

Doing your own patent requires considerable diligence, but it can be done. The body of the patent, which is mainly background description including drawings and the specification that tells how the device is made, is not too difficult. By reading other patents that you have received as a result of your search, you will not only have a pretty good idea of the language and the style, but you can also copy, word for word, some of the background material. However, when you come to the claims section—the last page or so of every patent—here is where you may have difficulty.

Claims, as they are written into a patent, are nothing like advertising claims. They are more like the claims for a gold mine. A gold mine claim defines geographic boundaries, and a patent claim defines, in words, the boundaries of your invention's features compared to other patented inventions. To understand how to write claims, you must refer to *Patent It Yourself.*

If, after following Pressman's instructions, you feel that writing your own patent is too difficult, then you might consider doing the best you can at writing it and then have an agent or an attorney edit your writing. Or, write everything except the claims, and have an agent/attorney edit and write the claims. (Some, but not all, patent professionals are willing to work this way.) One caveat: If you write your own patent application without any professional help, your bargaining position with potential licensees may not be as strong as if it were professionally done.

Hire a Professional

As a general rule, if you are pressed for time, lack writing skills, and are not particularly strong at managing complex projects, you should think twice before drafting your own patent. The process is time-consuming—hours of reading to learn how to do it and many more hours to draft and monitor your application. Preparing and prosecuting your application (the technical term for shepherding an application through the USPTO) can easily use up 100-200 hours of your time.

For many, the expense of hiring a patent attorney ($4,000 to $10,000) is the biggest hurdle to filing a utility patent application. I will discuss methods of funding prosecution of your application in subsequent chapters.

The best way to get a referral to a good patent lawyer is to talk to other people who have actually used a particular lawyer's services. If you have an inventor "club" (nonprofit networking group) in your area, join it and ask for guidance on a good patent professional. Find the closest inventor group in your area by visiting the United Inventors Association website (www.uiausa.org) or phoning their administrator. See Chapter 12 for more information.

Keep in mind that one reason patents are expensive is because lawyers are expensive. But a lawyer is not needed to prepare and file a patent application. You can hire a patent agent to do it for you. Patent agents are usually less expensive than patent attorneys.

What's the difference? A patent agent has passed only the "patent bar" examination—that part of the law that deals only with the patenting process—and is not a full attorney. He or she cannot represent you in court. You never want to litigate in any event. The present cost to litigate a patent all the way to the appeals court in Washington, DC is around a million dollars—often more. Because patent agents need only the one degree (in a technical discipline), they usually are not able to command the high price that an attorney does. Most patent agents charge from half to two-thirds the hourly rate of an attorney. Always ask their hourly rate, and compare it with a patent attorney in the same locale.

A patent attorney is a full attorney who specializes in patent writing and/or litigation. He or she must have a degree in one of the technical disciplines, such as mechanical or electrical engineering, chemistry, and so on, and must have passed the patent bar and state bar in order to be licensed to practice before the U.S Patent & Trademark Office. This double discipline is why attorneys can charge their high hourly fees, which run from around $150 in the smaller cities to as much as $400 in the larger ones. Patent lawyers who litigate may charge even more.

To find either patent agents or patent attorneys, go to the Patent Office website (www.uspto.gov) and look for their listing by state.

Whether you use an agent or an attorney depends not only on their hourly rate but also on how you feel about the person when you meet. Most such professionals do not charge for an introductory meeting, at which you have the opportunity to ask the questions that will help you in your selection. Here are the questions that may save you several hundred dollars:

- What is your hourly rate?
- How long do you expect to take writing my regular patent application or provisional patent application (PPA)? (See "The Provisional Patent Application," above.)
- If I opt for the PPA, will it be inexpensively converted to a regular application at some later time? Will all of the writing except for claims (not needed in the PPA) be the same as for the regular application?
- What other costs can I anticipate?
- Can I pay you in increments, such as one-third when you have written the first draft, one-third when you file, and one-third when the patent issues?
- Are you willing to work with me if I attempt to write some of the application other than claims? (Or, will you review my PPA if I write it

myself, and, if so, how much will you charge me?)

You don't have to work with a local patent professional if your written definition and drawings are clear. I work with a patent agent who is a thousand miles from where I live, and I receive excellent work. You can usually find reputable patent professionals in *Inventors' Digest* magazine. (See Chapter 12 for more resources.)

The worst way to locate a patent professional is to comb through advertisements or unscreened lists of lawyers provided by a local bar association (or the phone company). Local bar associations often maintain and advertise lawyer referral services. However, a lawyer can usually get on this list simply by volunteering. Very little (if any) screening is done to find out whether the lawyers are any good. Similarly, advertisements in the yellow pages, in newspapers, on television, or online say nothing meaningful about a lawyer's skills or manner—just that he could afford to pay for the ad.

If you are having difficulty locating an attorney knowledgeable about inventions and patent law, check out the American Intellectual Property Law Association (AIPLA), at www.aipla.org, or the Intellectual Property Law Association of the American Bar Association, at www.abanet.org. The USPTO website (www.uspto.gov) also maintains a list of attorneys and patent agents licensed to practice before the USPTO.

Keeping Attorney Fees Down

Patent and intellectual property attorneys generally charge $200 to $400 per hour, and preparing and filing an application can cost anywhere from $4,000 to $10,000. To save yourself a lot of money and grief, follow these tips.

Keep it short. If you are paying your attorney on an hourly basis, keep your conversations short—the meter is always running. Avoid making several calls a day; instead, consolidate your questions and ask them all in one conversation.

Get a fee agreement. Always get a written fee agreement when dealing with an attorney. Read it and make sure you understand it. Your fee agreement should give you the right to an itemized billing statement that details the work done and time spent.

Watch out for hidden expenses. Find out what expenses you will have to pay. Hopefully you can avoid an attorney that bills for services like word processing. (This means you will be paying the secretary's salary.) Also beware of exorbitant fax and copying charges.

Remember, you can always fire your lawyer. (You're still obligated to pay outstanding bills, though.) If you don't respect and trust your attorney's professional abilities, you should find a new attorney.

 Issued patents always list the inventor's attorney. If you notice, while searching through prior art, that many of the patents in your field were prepared by the same attorney, you may want to consider contacting that attorney. The lawyer is likely to be familiar with the field and the prior art.

Patent Alternatives

For inventors seeking to license their creation for royalties, the patent is almost always essential, while entrepreneurial inventors may have ways to gain exclusivity other than a patent. Before patenting, consider the following strategies:

- **First to market.** If you are an entrepreneurial inventor selling your product through catalogs, you gain exclusivity of sorts by being the first to get most of the appropriate catalog houses to take on your product. This first-to-market strategy is especially important if your product has a short shelf life. It often takes up to two years to acquire a patent, and you cannot stop infringers until you acquire one. Therefore, a patent may be useless for a product whose sales are over within two Christmas seasons. It is possible for a second supplier to bump you if he offers a much higher profit margin, but you will generally have an opportunity to adjust your pricing before a switch takes place. This same effect holds true for "bricks and glass" retailers, but to a lesser extent. Many retail stores carry competing lines, whereas catalogers generally want only one of a kind in their catalog.

- **Niche product.** The smaller the market for your product, the less attractive it will be for a competitor to "tool up" to produce and market a competing model. Even if there is easy entry in the market by a second source, a potential competitor must always assess whether the total cost of entry will be paid off by sufficient sales volume. Suppose that you do have a competitor. Two suppliers in a small market isn't always a bad situation. A small market, by its nature, usually cannot popularize its product effectively. A second source helps to advertise the product, and, in some cases, sales go up for each of the competitors.

- **Exclusive distribution.** It's unfortunate but true that many, probably most, new products coming from small inventor startup companies are not welcomed by established retailer buyers. (Catalog houses are the exception. Their businesses are built on cottage industries.) Retail buyers don't want to deal with a product line that contains only one product—especially a product that they consider a minor contribu-

tion to their profit. So, the inventor must often "piggy-back" his or her invention with a manufacturer/distributor that offers a complementary line of products. For example, the inventor of a new type of pizza cutter may enter into an exclusive branding distribution agreement with a frozen pizza maker. In this case, a patent may not necessarily be necessary if you can acquire a substantial volume and an exclusive distribution arrangement.

- **Trade secret protection.** Any confidential information about your invention which is not known by competitors and gives you an advantage over competitors is considered a trade secret. In order to maintain ownership rights over a trade secret, you must treat this information with secrecy—for example, the way the Coca-Cola Company treats the formula for Coke. Any public disclosure will end trade secrecy status for the information, and anyone will be free to use it. Some inventors choose to protect their inventions under trade secret law rather than under patent law. The cost of trade secret protection is minimal, and it does not involve a public disclosure program (such as used by the U.S. Patent Office). But there is a downside to choosing trade secret protection. To stop an infringer of your trade secret, you must be able to demonstrate (1) that you have treated the secret with confidentiality and (2) that the infringer acquired the secret through improper means. If it can be proven that you disclosed the information without confidentiality—even to someone other than the infringer—or that the information was legitimately "reverse engineered" (someone disassembles your invention) or independently developed, then you will not able to stop a competitor. On the other hand, trade secret protection will last as long as the secret is kept confidential. For example, some formulas and methods have been kept secret for decades. For more on trade secrets, see the resources provided in Chapter 12.

- **Trademark protection.** There are many devices that protect against auto theft, but if you asked most consumers to provide the name of one anti-theft product, they'd probably name "The Club", an invention that attaches to a steering wheel and prevents it from moving. Consumers remember "The Club" because it has been marketed aggressively. When a name, logo, or other indicia creates an association for consumers—usually as a result of advertising—that

name functions as a trademark, and the owner can stop competitors from using a similar name. A trademark can be registered (the USPTO has automated the process at its website). You can also reserve a trademark for future use provided you have a bona fide intention to use it in connection with your invention. Trademark protection outlasts patent protection (trademarks can last forever; a patent expires 20 years from the filing date) and, for that reason, trademarks provide a means of continued income after patent protection. For example, the patents for the Lego toys ended in 1978, but the Danish company that owns the construction toy has been pursuing competitors under trademark laws since that time. In other words, even though you can no longer stop someone from copying your invention, you *can* stop them from using your trademarked name. There's lot of free information on trademarks at the USPTO website, and you can learn more by reviewing *Trademark: Legal Care for Your Business & Product Name,* by Steve Elias (Nolo).

- **The Provisional Patent Application (PPA).** The provisional patent application is really an alternative to a patent, but it is included here because it provides a much less expensive method (compared to a patent filing) of holding your place in line in the patent office for one year. It's also far less demanding than a regular patent application. No claims are required, and a patent examiner doesn't review the application. The PPA establishes your date of invention, but if you don't follow through within one year with your regular application, you lose any benefit of the filing date. The main advantage of a PPA, in my opinion, is that you can legally state "patent applied for" or "patent pending" on your prototype, on your product (if you are that far along), and in descriptive matter on brochures (and so on) for the year that the PPA is valid. In short, it buys you a year before you are required to file a regular patent application. Many agents or attorneys who write PPAs will write them so that they form the entire body of your eventual regular patent application, and if you decide to go ahead with the regular application, all that is needed is to add the claims. If you do use the PPA approach, be sure to discuss this last point with your agent or attorney, and make sure the PPA is written so that it forms the body of your eventual regular application. Most PPAs will cost between half and 80 percent of the

cost of a regular application. If you write your own PPA, the disadvantage, other than those mentioned above, is that if you don't do a good job of thoroughly describing your invention and clearly teaching how it is made, your PPA will not be honored by the patent examiner for its filing date if and when you need to rely on its date. This is usually not too serious. However, if another inventor filed after the filing date of your defunct PPA and before you filed your regular patent application, that inventor would probably prevail and get the patent. So be sure to cover every detail in describing your invention. And if you change your invention (add one or more features) after your filing, then file another PPA with the changes incorporated. For more on provisional patent application resources, see Chapter 12.

Test Market Your Invention

Sophocles said, "Knowledge must come through action; you can have no test which is not fanciful, save by trial."

Whether you plan to license or produce, you will learn much from testing the market with a limited production run. Test marketing is different from assessing marketability. Market assessments are projections and calculations based on standardized criteria. In a test marketing scenario, potential users or customers actually handle and judge your invention and provide feedback.

The inventor who plans to license may chose to avoid test marketing because of the additional time and cost. Positive market results make it easier to license an invention, of course. But this is an optional step. If you plan to produce your invention, results from test marketing, if good, are compelling when you solicit an investor. This means that you probably will have to invest in more advanced tooling than that used to produce your prototype.

To test your product on the market, try to work a deal with a local merchant. You will have to price your product at a figure that your potential customers will feel is equal to or lower than its perceived value. Perceived value is the key. No one cares how much your product costs you to make. And you almost certainly will have to sacrifice profit on such testing—maybe even lose money. Edison sold his first light bulbs for a lot less than his cost in order to satisfy his customer's perceived value.

If your product can be sold through catalogs, you will have to produce a certain quantity as samples for the catalog houses. There are more than 15,000 catalog houses in the U.S., and this is an inventor-friendly market. Catalogs thrive on innovative products that are not yet sold through regular retail channels.

If you are uncertain about how to proceed to test the market, you might consider talking to the marketing chair at your nearby university for guidance. Universities regularly work with manufacturers to test market products. This is the way they create real situations for their students.

Tooling and Molds

Full production tooling is almost always expensive. A typical plastic injection mold, for example, may cost $25,000 if made in the United States. But for nearly every production process there is a spectrum of tooling—several choices that will be appropriate for ranges of quantities from one to a million or more. For example, if one of your key components is molded from plastic, your prototype may have been made by machining a solid chunk of plastic. If you decide to make ten or twenty pieces, a silicone rubber mold can be made from a master pattern, and a two-part liquid resin can be cast in such mold. If you wish to make 200 pieces, or 2000, you may find that a single-cavity aluminum mold is economical at $4,000. And when you go into full production, a four-cavity steel mold at $25,000 is economical. Be sure to understand this principle. I have dealt with several inventors who have bought expensive production tooling in order to produce a prototype or a few pieces. The tooling vendor should have turned the job away and guided the inventor to one of the low-volume processes. But tooling vendors are specialists and don't always know about the other processes. And some do know, but greed gets in the way of their doing the right thing.

Each unit produced on small-volume tooling will be more expensive than when you or your licensee produce larger quantities for the regular market. In the case of a single-cavity mold, the cost per piece may be $1.00. When you produce using the four-cavity mold, the cycle time will be the same as for the single-cavity mold, and the cost per piece will drop dramatically. For example, if the $1.00 cost consists of 12 cents material and 88 cents machine cycle time cost, the four-cavity price per unit will be 12 cents material and 22 cents machine cycle time cost (88 cents divided by 4), for a total of 34 cents—about one-third the single-cavity cost per unit.

The best way to find the right method is to solicit prices and ask questions. Vendors may know their own machines and processes intimately but are often not familiar with the processes and machines that serve volumes smaller and larger than the volume served economically by their facility.

If you can find a seasoned manufacturing engineer, perhaps at one of the universities, consult with this person on the process and tooling options for making your small-production run tooling. If this is not practical, spend a lot of time asking questions and getting prices. Another option is to purchase a copy of *Design for Manufacturability Handbook* (McGraw Hill Professional), by James G. Bralla.

Chapter 4

Self-Financing Your Idea

Here's a rule of finance: If you have not placed your own money at risk, you will have a harder time attracting financing.

Before you beg, borrow, or otherwise acquire money from private investors, I must emphasize one of the main principles of financing a great idea in the early stages: Potential investors shy away from investment opportunities in which the inventor has little or no financial interest.

The creative person who merely dreams up a "great idea" and expects that the idea alone is his or her contribution to a venture is either arrogant or naive. Am I too harsh? So be it. Go out and prove me wrong. You can only establish credibility with your prospects by personally having "suffered." You've got to bleed a little and show a few scars to prove that you really believe in your venture.

You may think that your personal financial condition is none of the investor's business. Although some inventors get lucky and acquire small investments (one to two thousand dollars) without disclosure, it is quite common for an investor to require a full financial disclosure before providing serious money. Often that means furnishing the same type of documentation—tax returns or other proof of earnings—as required for bank loans.

You may also feel that having the idea and developing it on paper is a sufficient contribution. But as much as you may dream of an investor who will pay for everything—from the earliest expenses to production invention—it will not happen unless you take a financial gamble on your idea.

This principle holds for all levels of investment, whether a thousand dollars for a marketability assessment and patent search or a million dollars for production expansion. If the inventor has little or nothing to lose, the investor sees a red flag and is likely to walk away at a brisk pace.

The total dollar amount of your investment is less important than its relativity to your net worth. For example, if you own your own home and your mortgage is half paid, your investor will wonder why you haven't borrowed against this equity and financed your early-stage expenses yourself. Be prepared for the fact that you must show your potential investor that you have put in as much of your own money as you can without jeopardizing your family's essentials—that is, you are willing to "bleed" a little for the sake of investment.

Making this investment may prove to be a difficult decision. How much can you really afford to invest? Will your spouse or partner object to this use? This is a matter you must discuss with your family and perhaps your financial adviser. But, as part of your discussion, you'll need to assess how much money is required and what the money will be used for.

As explained in Chapter 1, the early stages of invention and innovation are

You Can Deduct Your Inventing Expenses

There is some "good" news, however, and that is that you may be able to deduct your inventing expenses from your ordinary income.

To qualify for a deduction, you must satisfy three basic requirements:

- **You must be in the "inventing" business.** Inventing qualifies as a business for tax purposes only if (1) you work at it regularly, and (2) your primary motive for doing it is to earn a profit. If the IRS concludes you have some other motive for inventing, you cannot claim the deduction.

- **You must keep records of your expenses.** You need to keep records of these expenses to (1) know for sure how much you actually spent and (2) prove to the IRS you really incurred the expenses listed on your tax return in the event you're audited, and

- **You must have a legal basis for the deduction.** Inventors are fortunate in that the tax law gives them more ways to deduct their expenses than are available to most businesspeople. It is usually not necessary to indicate on your tax return which tax law provision you're relying on for a deduction. But, if you're audited by the IRS, you'll have to provide a legal basis for all your deductions. If the IRS concludes you lack such a basis, it will deny the deduction and you'll have to pay back taxes and penalties. If, like most independent inventors, you're a sole proprietor, your deductions will be listed on IRS Schedule C, Profit or Loss From Business.

typically financed by what is called gas money and seed money. Both the inventor-for-royalties and the entrepreneurial inventor have to find their gas money and seed money without the benefit of a fair-size bank loan unless they are willing to pledge an asset, such as real estate, as collateral for such loan.

That means you will likely have to use money from personal sources such as savings, credit cards, small signature loans, loans against life insurance, and life insurance dividends. These sources are discussed in more detail later in this chapter.

 For more information on tax rules for inventors, read *What Every Inventor Needs to Know About Business & Taxes*, by Stephen Fishman (Nolo).

Savings

Personal savings is the surest, safest, and least-encumbered source for financing an invention. If you have savings available for invention financing, great. But you should use it carefully and methodically. Always keep in mind that many inventions have obvious merit and serve a real need, but they cannot always be marketed profitably. Therefore, don't risk savings if during your second task in preparation (assessing marketability) you learn the discouraging news from a professional evaluation that you cannot market your invention.

Sometimes the greatest savings of all occurs by not spending more money on your invention. You can preserve your money for future inventions, or, as the old English proverb goes, "He who fights and runs away may live to fight another day."

If you haven't acquired any savings and your invention doesn't demand a panic response—that is, you're not racing against other inventors to get the product to the patent office and to market—you may find a distinct advantage in accumulating savings for the specific purpose of financing the early stages of your invention.

I'll try not to bore you with the obvious here. But sometimes we overlook that which is apparent. For example, you probably have a checking account. You may even have a savings account that is part of your bank's account package. Are you using it? Unless you are transferring a fixed amount to your savings account with each regular deposit to your checking account, you aren't doing justice to your venture. If you really plan to succeed with your invention, devote a fraction of your earnings to a savings account—even $20 a week will get you a thousand dollars in a year. And do this habitually, even though you may give up on your present invention. If you are an inventor by nature, you will come up with another invention in the near future, and you will need the money that you are dedicating to rightful personal fulfillment.

The gradual accumulation of money is not the only benefit of routine savings. Each time you become consciously aware of your savings account, you are affirming to your subconscious mind that you really do plan to succeed with your invention. And, by dedicating a fixed amount each payday, you automatically reduce the amount budgeted for all other expenses, thereby disciplining yourself and your family to restrict elective spending in ways that are acceptable and supportive of your goal. If an emergency arises, you still have the savings available. If it's smooth sailing, you'll have your gas money or seed money in less than a year.

Credit Cards

A survey by Arthur Anderson indicated that one-third of all small business respondents used credit cards for the initial funding of their startup. Credit cards are a simple source of financing—provided you are able to pay them off. When you consider that in the U.S. the average consumer has access to $12,190 from credit cards, it's tempting to pay for most of the basic expenses detailed in the previous chapter with plastic. If you plan to do this, keep in mind that you could be stuck with that credit card for a long time. If you make the minimum payments, for example, it's not uncommon that it could take a decade or more to pay off a credit card debt.

As you're also probably aware, credit card companies often use high interest rates and extraordinary penalties. In addition, you may be tempted to get cash advances to pay for invention expenses. This is particularly troublesome for three reasons: (1) you will pay higher interest; (2) you will pay transaction fees; and (3) you will not get a grace period (which means you pay interest from the day you make the purchase, even if you pay off your balance in full).

Definitely stay away from credit cards if you are the kind of person who always runs a high balance on your credit card. For example, if all of your credit card balances are greater than 80 percent of your credit limits, stay away from cards—you've got a problem. Calculate your debt-to-income ratio. Divide your total monthly debt payment (excluding mortgage/rent) by your total monthly gross income (before taxes). You've got a problem if your debt-to-income ratio is near or over 20 percent.

Invention expenses, even if carefully budgeted, will almost always be higher than planned. Use your credit cards only when an invention emergency arises. Save your available credit for your personal needs. I have known inventors who have caused great discord in their marriages due to irresponsible use of their credit cards. Always remember, too, that the credit bureaus know how you use and pay back the expenditures that you charge against your cards. Your ability to eventually borrow or gain investment from other sources is influenced by your credit card management. Credit card companies also keep track of how many credit cards you have, and their balances. Big Brother is always watching.

Signature Loans

Small signature loans are often available from your bank based on your credit rating and your history with the bank. (The name refers to the fact that a consumer may get a loan offer in the mail or from a bank and all that is required is the consumer's signature to make it binding.) If your credit history is good, and you are buying your own home, you can often get a few thousand dollars without pledging collateral. However, beware that many banks and credit unions have moved away from signature loans and are being replaced in this market by signature loans from large financial conglomerates such as GE Financial. Signature loans are sometimes made under conditions known as predatory lending. Read Chapter 5, before making a signature loan.

Loans Against Life Insurance

Check your life insurance policy. After a time certain types of life insurance

policies—for example, whole life, permanent life, and variable universal life policies—permit you to borrow against policy reserves. You may have accumulated a surprising amount of value (or, in some cases, you may find that cash value has diminished as a result of poorly performing investments made by the insurance company). You can also cancel these policies and obtain the cash surrender value, but that decision is not one you should make lightly. Consider your age, family obligations, and ability to reacquire life insurance, as well as the size of the cash surrender penalty, if any, before cashing out.

Life Insurance Dividends

Some forms of life insurance pay dividends that remain on deposit until you withdraw them. Check your policy, or phone your insurance company to find out if your insurance has residual value that you can withdraw without degrading the quality of your insurance. Beware, however, that all dividends are not equal. Many people who bought whole life insurance policies in the 1990s were lead to believe that they would eventually be earning dividends high enough to cover the annual premium. Alas, things didn't work as planned, and changing interest rates forced many insurers to cut dividends.

Personal Sacrifice as a Financing Tool

Some inventors manage to find gas money and seed money in the strangest places—for example, a closet, garage, or attic. Many of us love to buy electronic toys and comfort items and later find that these temporarily loved products have been relegated to storage. The amazing growth of the personal storage facilities all over the country attests to this problem.

Try this: Take everything out of your largest closet, and lay it on the floor. Can't some of this be sold at a garage sale, on Ebay, or at a flea market? When my elderly next-door neighbor died, her children arranged a yard sale and sold hundreds of items, most of which the mother could have parted with before she died. The yard sale—including cookware, dishes and glasses, furniture, knickknacks, tools, and all kinds of odds and ends—netted over $3,000. Considering that the average weekend yard sale brings in $300 to $500, there's money to finance some step in the invention process—and it frees up space in your home.

And what about that stamp or coin collection that you have tucked away on the top shelf of your closet? You haven't looked at it in years. Can it be converted to cash? Selling your stuff via Ebay is an easy way to finance your invention.

Alternatively, you should ask, "What type of belt-tightening can I do to reduce household expenses?" You need to be creative and think outside of the box.

One area to consider is food and diet. Most of us can easily cut our food bills down by at least $20 a week without feeling deprived. Start by not changing anything immediately and keeping very accurate totals of your weekly food expenses, including the expense of eating out. Then, set a budget with a maximum of $20 per week less than your past average total. Or, consider healthy eating as a means of saving money. By getting more of your protein from grains and legumes and less from animals, you'll spend significantly less money—money that can be devoted to your invention. And current thinking is that you'll be doing your general health, especially your heart, a favor as well.

What about your car? It's nice to have a new one every so often, but is it necessary? A $500 repair bill once or twice a year is a lot less expensive than $250 to $300 paid out every month. Here is $2,000 saved annually in addition to at least the $1,000 that you are already saving from your food budget, and the $1,000 in your banked savings.

You get the idea. Which do you really want: comfortable complacency, or your invention driven to success?

Borrowing From Family and Friends

This can be sticky. The golden rule for getting money from family and friends is simple: Don't borrow. Instead, form a small corporation or limited liability company, and sell shares. (I discuss the corporate investor in more detail in Chapter 5.) Inform your investors that they will own part of your company, and that all inventions—even seemingly sure things—have a high degree of risk. Explain that if your invention pays off, it may pay off handsomely for each and all. If it fails, everybody loses. Will this cause a few potential investors to hold back? Sure. Your old granny living on Social Security may not feel comfortable in buying into your venture. But you'll surely have an easier time approaching your financially comfortable friends and relatives with a business proposition than you would if you had hoped to borrow. And, more important, if your venture fails, you won't have nearly the embarrassment about not being able to pay back loans. People like an intelligent gamble; they hate to lend money. (If you do borrow from friends or relatives, consider CircleLending.com (www.circlelending .com), a loan facilitator, discussed in Chapter 5.)

■

Chapter 5

Lenders and Investors

Contributions to your venture come in two forms. In one form, someone lends you money, and, under the terms of the loan agreement (sometimes referred to as the "note"), you are obligated to repay the amount borrowed (the "principal") along with interest. The other common method of acquiring money is when someone makes an investment in your enterprise and in return acquires a partial ownership (usually in the form of stock in your corporation).

In most cases, the person (or institution) with the money will make the decision whether to lend you the money (debt financing) or invest (equity financing). For example, banks traditionally loan money, and venture capitalists traditionally acquire equity. In some cases, you may deal with someone who loans money *and* invests. Whichever is chosen, the distinction between debt and equity will have an important effect on the development of your invention business. This chapter explains the basic principles of debt and equity financing.

Loans

Imagine seeing a sign on a bank that reads, "We can loan you enough money to get you completely out of debt." Sometimes— for example, when considering credit card offers—it really seems like banks honestly believe this marketing ploy. Alas, the reality is that whenever you borrow, you will always go deeper into debt.

Borrowing: The Basics

A loan is commonly backed by your promise to pay back the amount with interest. Interest—the sweetener for the person risking the money—is only one of the factors working against borrowers. Your loan may be secured by your property—for example, your home or car—or you may be obligated personally (known as a "personal guarantee"). In subsequent chapters information is provided on different types and sources of loans. If you are unfamiliar with loan terminology, here are a few important terms:

- **Amortization.** Lenders have developed formulas for calculating interest and repayment of principal into a neat monthly payment. It's referred to as amortization, and it's the system by which the total liability of the loan—interest and principal—is calculated and paid off over a period of time. A "fully amortized" loan is one in which you make equal monthly payments over a period of months, at the end of which the loan is fully paid off. If you wanted to calculate the difference between a 10% and a 12% interest rate, you can use one of the many amortization calculators found on the Internet.
- **Prepayment penalty.** Some entrepreneurs may be fortunate enough to pay back the loan before the time set in the note. Here's the catch: Some state laws allow repayment

of the entire principal at any time with no penalty, but some states permit lenders to charge a penalty (to compensate for lost interest). Prepayment penalties can sometimes be so hefty that it makes prepayment a futile gesture. Check out any prepayment penalties before signing a loan.

- **Balloon payment loan.** This type of arrangement (sometimes known as an "interest only" loan) allows for relatively small monthly payments, usually consisting only of interest payments, followed by a single large payment that usually covers the principal.

- **Personal guarantees.** Many lenders are happy to lend money to a business provided that an individual personally guarantees the loan. If you personally guarantee a debt, you will be personally liable for any judgment resulting from a default. Unfortunately, this is a common requirement for many commercial loans. Keep in mind that if you personally guarantee the loan, having an LLC or a corporation won't protect you from creditors if you default, even if your business goes into bankruptcy. (It would only be affected if you declared personal bankruptcy).

- **Secured loans (collateral).** Sometimes the loan is "secured", which means that you must pledge some

property as part of the loan agreement—for example, the bank may take a second mortgage on your house. If you fail to honor the loan agreement—for example, you miss several payments—the lender can acquire the secured property (known as "collateral") and sell it off to recover the amount due on the loan.

Advantages and Disadvantages of Borrowing Money

The major advantage of a loan is that it is not an investment. In other words, you are not giving up any ownership in your enterprise. For that reason, some business people prefer borrowing money to giving up a piece of the business. With a loan, all you have to do is pay the money back. You still maintain ownership of everything. In addition, the interest payments are a deductible business expense, and, sometimes, when borrowing from friends or family you can get more reasonable repayment terms.

The obvious disadvantage of a loan is the debt—the looming monthly payments and the potential for personal liability (if you guaranteed the loan), loss of property (if you secured the loan), or potential for a lawsuit if you default on the loan payments. In a worst-case scenario—one in which you secured the loan or guaranteed it—your failure default could result in the loss of your invention rights, attachment of your wages, or a judgment that can be used against your property.

Most business experts recommend against financing your enterprise solely with borrowed money, and many experts suggest avoiding financing more than half of your enterprise with borrowed money. Loans are best when you have a realistic expectation that you will be able to pay off the loans—that is, a predictable cash flow.

Since your tax situation is affected by borrowing, always consult your accountant or tax preparer before assuming debt financing. For information about loans from banks and other financial institutions, review Chapter 10.

 CircleLending: a "safer" way to borrow from friends and family. If you're taking a loan from friends, relatives, or other third parties, check out CircleLending.com (www.circlelending. com). CircleLending doesn't lend money —it facilitates loans. A CircleLending loan specialist examines your loan, helps to prepare a legally binding agreement (with secured collateral, if required), and then creates a repayment schedule. The company also manages the payment process through automatic electronic debits and credits and will send payment reminders to the borrower. The company will even restructure the loan if required. CircleLending must be doing something right. Their default rate is 5%, compared with 14% for comparable unstructured loans.

Avoid Predatory Lenders

Predatory lending is any unfair credit practice that harms the borrower or supports a credit system that promotes inequality and poverty. The most common predatory lending practices occur in the subprime loan market. Traditionally, a subprime lender provided high-interest loans to borrowers with bad credit or no credit history—those who do not qualify for the prime market. In some cases, subprime lending was necessary; after all, if someone is a higher credit risk, then it's not abnormal to charge higher interest on loans. However, what is happening more regularly these days is that you may qualify for prime lender rates but are being unfairly derailed into subprime loans that use some of predatory lending practices described below:

- **Pay a higher interest rate.** Every lender has a set of underwriting guidelines that determine the interest rate by assessing a borrower's risk. The most common predatory practice is to place a borrower into a higher-interest-rate (subprime) loan than the credit risk would call for. For example, you may qualify for a 6.5% prime loan, but the lender charges you a 10% subprime rate. Brokers and loan "originators" often get bonuses for placing borrowers into higher rates, so there's a great incentive to act in a predatory manner. You don't have to accept the interest rate offered. Seek more than one opinion on your borrowing status, and keep in mind that studies by Freddie Mac and Standard & Poor's indicate that 63 percent of subprime borrowers would have qualified for conventional "A" or "A-" prime quality loans.

- **Charge exorbitant fees.** In addition to channeling you into more expensive loans, predatory lenders often charge exorbitant fees. For example, a predatory subprime loan may include a 10% "loan origination" fee. There are also exorbitant penalty fees if you try to pay the loan off early. Why make it so hard to pay off the loan? Because these lenders make a lot of money by bundling their loans and selling them to insurance companies, pension plans, mutual funds, and other investors. If the borrower can't pay off the loan, that makes it more attractive on this secondary market. As a general rule, a loan in which the fees exceed five percent of the loan is probably predatory and you should avoid it, if possible.

- **Charge outrageous fees for life insurance.** If you should die, a credit life insurance policy would pay off some—but probably not all—of the principal left on the loan. Sometimes these life insurance policies are only good for the first five years of the policy, but the payments are spread over the life of the loan (20 or 30

years). If you want credit life insurance for your loan, shop around for the best deal, and avoid paying for it all up front (often by deducting the amount from your equity). The lender has little incentive to provide you with good life insurance rates, since lenders are affiliated with or own a credit life insurance company and want to land the higher rates.

- **Switch the paperwork.** Quite often, the most deceptive predatory lending tactic is to switch the terms of the loan after the initial agreement is made between the lender and borrower. The borrower signs paperwork for fees and interest rates that were not agreed upon. Don't be pressured into signing documentation without reading it.

Avoiding predatory loan practices is often easier said than done. First of all, many of the practices described above are legal in all states except North Carolina, unless the lender is acting this way as part of a discriminatory scheme—for example, only overcharging members of a minority group, the elderly, or others protected by law. In the case of discriminatory pricing schemes—for example, black borrowers are systematically charged higher rates than white borrowers with similar credit history—a borrower may make claims under the Fair Housing Act of 1968 and the Equal Credit Opportunity Act of 1972. However, in reality, these laws are not often enforced despite the fact, as explained below, that statistics demonstrate that discrimination is present.

Second, many small businesses secure loans via the home mortgage market, which are, unfortunately, issuing fewer and fewer home mortgages. As this prime loan market deflates, the subprime market—with its much higher profit margin—is growing wildly.

Third, despite a prohibition against discriminatory practices, studies by HUD indicate that the proportion of approved white prime loans versus disapproved loans to black and Hispanic borrowers is increasing dramatically, forcing minorities into the subprime market.

Finally, though banks that operate as prime lenders may be subject to some scrutiny under the Community Reinvestment Act (CRA) of 1976 (which allows community groups to hold banks accountable for their lending to minority and low-wealth neighborhoods), the federal regulation does not affect subprime lenders owned by those banks. It's no wonder, for example, that Bank of America is the largest subprime lender in the country or that Wells Fargo owns three subprime lenders.

In September 2002, Citigroup agreed to pay $240 million to settle accusations that CitiFinancial, one of the country's largest subprime lenders, used deceptive practices to sell home loan insurance to customers with a history of unpaid debts.

Since there is so little federal or state regulation of these predatory lending practices, the burden is on you to avoid these practices. Bottom line: It's not worth financing your invention with a predatory loan that will drag down your personal finances.

Equity Financing— Seeking Investment

Investors are gamblers. They will look at your invention as if it were a hand dealt in a game of poker and decide, based on the odds of business, whether this hand is likely to be a winner. If they share your excitement, believe in the potential, and understand the odds, they may buy into your hand. That, in a nutshell, is equity financing. Someone is willing to gamble on becoming a part-owner of your enterprise.

Will people really invest in your invention business? Yes. There is a touch of wishful thinking in most of us—a spirit of adventure—even healthy greed. There is a part of our psyche that is supremely satisfied whenever the bells ring and the coins come gushing out of the slot machine. Even when we know the odds are stacked against us, we still play for the anticipated thrill of winning the long shot. Lotto depends on it. Casinos depend on it. And we inventors can harness this mysterious aspect of human nature in order to fund our ventures.

Offering Stock?
The Government Is Watching

The law treats corporate shares, limited partnership interests, and (usually) passive LLC membership interests as securities. Federal and state securities laws regulate the issuance of these securities to investors.

This means that before you sell equity to an investor, you'll need to learn more about securities laws requirements. Fortunately, there are generous exemptions that normally allow a small business to provide a limited number of investors an interest in the business without complicated paperwork. In the rare cases in which your business won't qualify for these exemptions, you have to comply with the complex disclosure requirements of the securities laws—such as distributing an approved prospectus to potential investors—and register the securities. In this case, it may be too much trouble to do the deal unless a great deal of money is involved.

Even if you qualify for exemptions to the securities disclosure rules, investors may eventually accuse you of giving them misleading assurances. Always recommend (in writing, preferably) that potential investors check with their own financial and legal advisers to evaluate the investment. The bottom line is that, although each investor will assess his or her own degree of risk, you should disclose all the relevant information to them so they can make an intelligent, informed choice. More information about these SEC rules is provided in Chapter 9.

Equity and Innovation

Your attorney, accountant, and other advisers can help you structure equity investments in creative ways. For example, one business took a $5 million equity investment on the condition that the first $5 million in profits would go to the investor. After that, profits would be divided between the investor and the CEO (and founder) of the business according to a sliding scale. If the business were to earn over $10 million a year, for two years the CEO would end up with more money than the investor. Even if the company didn't hit the desired numbers, the CEO still received a regular salary.

Business Forms and Investments

In order to accommodate equity financing, two things have to happen:

- You must convince the investor you have a worthwhile enterprise (more on that in Chapters 6 and 7).
- You must have a business entity that can accommodate investment—that is, you must do the paperwork with your partnership, limited liability company, or corporation to officially grant ownership interests to investors.

Below is a discussion of the various types of entities and how these grants of ownership are made.

Which is the best for you, an LLC, C corporation, or Subchapter S corporation? This depends on the regulations of the state in which you intend to incorporate. You should review the resources below and/or consult with an accountant and an attorney.

Partnership

A partnership is a business in which two or more owners agree to share profits (and losses). If you decide to go into business with another person, you have automatically formed a general partnership—even if you never signed a formal partnership agreement. A general partnership really can be started with a handshake (although it makes far more sense to prepare and sign a written partnership agreement. Each partner is personally liable for all business debts and any claims (including court judgments) against the partnership that the business can't pay. For example, if your business fails to pay its suppliers, the partners are personally responsible for paying these business debts and may have to mortgage their houses, sell their cars, and empty personal bank accounts to come up with the necessary cash.

And creditors don't have to respect the partners' internal arrangements about who owns what percentage of the company's assets or who is responsible for

what share of the partnership's debts. If the business owes money it can't pay, the creditor may go after any general partner for the entire debt, regardless of his or her partnership ownership percentage. (If this happens, the partner who is sued can in turn sue the other partners to force them to repay their shares of the debt, but this can be costly and time-consuming.)

Personal liability for business debts is even more worrisome, because each general partner may bind the entire partnership (and all of the partners) to a contract or business deal. In legal jargon, each partner is an agent of the partnership, with the right to undertake obligations on its behalf. (Fortunately, there are a few significant limitations to this agency rule—to be valid, a contract or deal must generally be within the scope of the partnership's business, and the outside person who makes the deal with a partner must reasonably think that the partner is authorized to act on behalf of the partnership.)

If a partnership can't fulfill a valid contract or other business deal, each partner may be held personally liable for the amount owed. This personal liability for the debts of the entire partnership, coupled with the agency authority of each partner to bind the others, makes the general partnership far riskier than entities such as LLCs, corporations, and limited partnerships, which offer at least some of the owners limited personal liability for business debts. Another factor to consider about partnerships is that owners pay business taxes on their individual income tax returns, just like sole proprietors (known as pass-through taxation).

A partnership is not an ideal business form for seeking investment from outsiders, as most investors will not want to take the personal liability risk. Nevertheless, if you wish to grant an equity interest in your partnership, you should enter into a written partnership agreement specifying each partner's ownership interest.

Limited Partnership

A limited partnership is similar to a general partnership, except it has two types of partners. A limited partnership must have at least one general partner, who manages the business and is personally liable for its debts and claims. (General partners have the same broad rights and responsibilities as the partners discussed in the general partnership section, above.) And, by definition, a limited partnership must also have at least one limited partner, and usually has more. A limited partner is typically the investor who contributes capital to the business but is not involved in day-to-day management. The limited partners are not personally liable for business debts and claims. They function much like passive shareholders in a small corporation, investing with the expectation of receiving a share of both profits and the eventual increase in the value of the business. For this reason, an investor is much more likely to invest in a limited partnership than in a general partnership.

As long as limited partners do not participate in management, they do not have personal liability for business debts and claims. However, if limited partners participate in decision making, this shield disappears, and they will be subject to personal liability for business debts.

For income tax purposes, limited partnerships generally are treated like general partnerships, with all partners individually reporting and paying taxes on their share of the profits each year.

As noted, limited partners are generally prohibited from managing the business. Some states have carved out some new exceptions to this ban, however, usually to allow a limited partner to vote on issues that affect the basic structure of the partnership, including the removal of general partners, terminating the partnership, amending the partnership agreement, or selling all or most of the assets of the partnership. If all owners want to be active in their company, they are better off forming an LLC or a corporation, which would allow all owners/investors to run the business while enjoying the protection of limited liability for business debts.

The limited partnership is generally considered to be less versatile than an LLC. Some companies still operate as limited partnerships for tax reasons—for example, your accountant determines that there are tax advantages in your state.

To create a limited partnership, you must pay an initial fee and file papers with the state—usually a "certificate of limited partnership." This document is similar to the articles (or certificate) filed by a corporation or an LLC and includes information about the general and limited partners. Filing fees are about the same for limited partnerships as for a corporation or an LLC.

Limited Liability Company (LLC)

The limited liability company (LLC) is popular with many small business owners, in part because it was designed by state legislatures to overcome limitations of each of the other business forms—including the corporation. Essentially, the LLC is a business ownership structure that allows owners to pay business taxes on their individual income tax returns like partners (or, for a one-person LLC, like a sole proprietorship) but that also gives the owners the legal protection of personal limited liability for business debts and judgments as if they had formed a corporation. So, an LLC provides both pass-through taxation of business profits (like a partnership) and limited personal liability for business debts (like a corporation). Under each state's LLC laws, the owners of an LLC are not personally liable for its debts and other liabilities. This personal legal liability protection is the same as that offered to shareholders of a corporation

Most LLCs are managed by all the owners (also called members). This is known as "member-management." But state law also allows for management by one or more specially appointed managers, who may be members or nonmembers. Not surprisingly (but somewhat awkwardly), this arrangement is known as "manager-management." In other words, an LLC can appoint one or more of its members, or one of its CEOs, or even a person contracted from outside the LLC, to manage its affairs. This manager setup is somewhat atypical; it makes sense only if one person wishes to assume full-time control of the LLC, while the other owners act as passive investors in the enterprise.

Like a corporation, it takes some paperwork to get an LLC going. You must file a legal document (usually called articles of organization) with the state business filing office. And if the LLC will maintain a business presence in another state, such as a branch office, you must also file registration or qualification papers with the other state's business filing office. LLC formation fees vary, but most are comparable to the fee each state charges for incorporation.

An investor in an LLC must abide by the rules of the operating agreement, which spell out how the LLC will be owned, how profits and losses will be divided, how departing or deceased members will be bought out, and other essential ownership details. If you don't prepare an operating agreement, the default provisions of the state's LLC Act will apply to the operation of your LLC. Because virtually all LLC owners will want to control exactly how profits and losses are apportioned among the members (as well as other essential LLC operating rules), you'll want to prepare an LLC operating agreement.

An LLC is a suitable vehicle for investors who will obtain limited liability. It's also more flexible in regard to payment of taxes. That said, many investors prefer the traditional advantages of a corporation as an investment vehicle, as described below.

LLCs and Securities Laws

If you'll be the sole owner of your LLC and you don't plan to take investments from outsiders, your ownership interest in the LLC will not be considered a "security," and you don't have to concern yourself with these laws. For co-owned LLCs, however, the answer to this question is not so clear.

First, let's consider the definition of a "security." A security is an investment in a profit-making enterprise that is not run by the investor. Here's another way to think about it: If a person invests in a business with the expectation of making money from the efforts of others, that person's investment is generally considered a "security" under federal and state law. Conversely, when a person will rely on his or her own efforts to make a profit (that is, he or she will be an active owner of an LLC), that person's ownership interest in the company will not usually be treated as a security.

How does this apply to you? Generally, if all of the owners will actively manage the LLC—the situation for most small startup LLCs—the LLC ownership interests will not be considered securities. But if one or more of your co-owners will not work for the company or play an active role in managing the company—as may be true for LLCs that accept investments from friends and family or that are run by a special management group—your LLC's ownership interests may be treated as securities by your state and by the federal Securities and Exchange Commission (SEC).

If your ownership interests are considered securities, you must get an exemption from the state and federal securities laws before the initial owners of your LLC invest their money. If you don't qualify for an exemption to the securities laws, you must register the sale of your LLC's ownership interests with the SEC and your state.

Fortunately, smaller LLCs, even those that plan to sell memberships to passive investors, usually qualify for securities law exemptions. For example, SEC rules exempt the private sale of securities if all owners reside in one state and all sales are made within the state; this is called the "intrastate offering" exemption. Another federal exemption covers "private offerings." A private offering is an unadvertised sale that is limited to a small number of people (35 or fewer) or to those who, because of their net worth or income earning capacity, can reasonably be expected to be able to take care of themselves in the investment process.

Most states have enacted their own versions of these popular federal exemptions.

For more information about SEC exemptions, visit the SEC website (www .sec.gov). A quick way to research your state's exemption rules is to go to the home page of your state's securities agency, which typically posts the state's exemptions rules and procedures. To find your state securities agency, go to your secretary of state's website. The Wyoming Secretary of State's office provides a list of state websites at http://soswy.state.wy .us/sos/sos2.htm.

Corporation

A corporation, like an LLC, is a statutory creature, created and regulated by state law. In short, if you want the "privilege"—that's what the courts call it—of turning your business enterprise into a corporation, you must follow the requirements of your state's business corporation law or business corporation act (BCA). What sets the corporation apart, in a theoretical sense, from all other types of businesses is that it is a legal and tax entity separate from any of the people who own, control, manage, or operate it.

Federal and state laws view the corporation as a legal "person," which means that the corporation can enter into its own contracts, incur its own debts, and pay its own taxes, separate and apart from its owners.

For tax purposes, there are two types of corporations: "C" corporations and

"S" corporations. A C corporation is just another name for a regular for-profit corporation—a corporation taxed under normal corporate income tax rules. The letter C comes from Subchapter C of the Internal Revenue Code and is used to distinguish these regular corporations from "S" corporations, a more specialized type of corporation that is regulated under Subchapter S of the Internal Revenue Code.

An S corporation gets the pass-through tax treatment of a partnership (with some important technical differences) and the limited liability of a corporation, much like an LLC. This section covers the more common and widely accepted C Corporation. (S corporations are discussed in more detail in this chapter.)

 LLCs have largely replaced S corporations. Formerly, the only way that all owners of a business could obtain personal liability protection while retaining pass-through taxation of business income was to form an S corporation. Since the advent of the LLC, however, S corporations have largely fallen out of favor. The LLC provides substantially the same benefits as an S corporation without several of the significant restrictions of S corporations. Since laws differ from state to state, consult with an attorney or accountant to determine the relative advantages of an LLC or S corporation in your state.

To form a corporation, you pay corporate filing fees and prepare and file formal organizational papers, usually called "articles of incorporation," with a state agency (in most states, the secretary or department of state). Once formed, the corporation assumes an independent legal life separate from its owners. This separate legal life leads to a number of familiar traditional corporate characteristics, discussed below

A corporation provides all of its owners —that is, its shareholders—with the benefits of limited personal liability protection. If a court judgment is entered against the corporation or the corporation can't pay its bills, only the corporation's assets are at stake. The shareholders stand to lose only the money that they've invested; creditors cannot go after their personal assets.

In an unincorporated business, the owners pay individual income taxes on all net profits of the business, regardless of how much they actually receive each year. For example, assume that a partnership or an LLC has two owners and earns $100,000 in net profits. If the owners split profits equally, each must report and pay individual income taxes on $50,000 of business profits. This is true even if all of the profits are kept in the business checking account to meet upcoming business expenses—not paid out to the owners.

In contrast, a corporation is a legal entity separate from its shareholders and files its own tax return, paying taxes on

any profits left in the business. Unlike most LLC members, shareholders who work for the corporation are treated as employees who receive salaries for their work in the business. The corporation deducts owners' salaries as a business expense when it computes its net taxable income. But because the owners of a small corporation also manage the business as its directors, they have the luxury of deciding how much to pay themselves in salary. In short, the owners decide how much of the profits will be taxed at the corporate level and how much will be paid out to them and taxed on their individual returns.

Two results follow from this:

- The owners pay individual income taxes only on salary amounts they actually receive, not on all the net profits of the business.
- The corporation—which, remember, is a separate tax entity—pays corporate taxes on the net profits actually retained in the business.

Corporations are the ideal means for making an investment. Shares can be issued to reflect ownership interests, and state laws provide for different level of stock ownership—for example, nonvoting and voting shares.

In general, when it comes to investment, there is something about owning speculative stock in a real corporation that appeals to the adventurous capitalist in most of us.

But isn't forming a corporation a little too pretentious for an invention? No, it isn't. Corporation law facilitates the formation of very small, liberally regulated corporations in most states, and the regulations allow for the sale of stock or other form of financial participation without a lot of complication and restrictions.

How does one go about setting up a small corporation? Start with a lawyer who specializes in setting up small corporations. Call several lawyers, and ask if they have specific experience in setting up corporations. You don't want a lawyer who works mainly with large corporations. The objectives, regulations, and advantages of large, as compared to small, corporations are distinctly different, and lawyers who work only or mainly with large corporations likely will be more expensive and may not be very dedicated to handling the "small potatoes" corporation like yours.

When preparing to distribute shares, deal with an attorney who is savvy about small business setups. You should not distribute shares in your company without a good understanding of how this will affect your ability to attract investors in the future. The generous inventor who sells too much stock to his relatives at bargain prices will find, later on, when he or she needs serious capital, that the angel will not be interested.

Your corporate attorney should advise you on this (and more information is provided in Chapters 8 and 9).

You can also contact SCORE (Service Corps of Retired Executives) through the Small Business Administration and ask to have free counseling from a retired investment banker, not a regular banker. You may even find your attorney through SCORE. The advice should be free, but you'll have to pay attorney fees for setting up your corporation. A retired attorney should be less expensive than one in current practice. Also contact the SBDCs (Small Business Development Centers) in your area.

Equity Financing: Advantages and Disadvantages

With equity financing, it is unlikely you will have to repay investors if your business goes under, and your personal property is unlikely to be at risk. Other advantages are that you often acquire advice and other types of help from those who have a vested interest in your business's success.

The major disadvantage of equity financing is that you get a smaller piece of the pie, since you are giving up a share of the business. You also may have several other cooks in the kitchen with you, offering advice and seeking information about events.

Considering the alternative—borrowing money—equity financing is often preferable because it reduces your financial risk and sometimes—with investor guidance—improves your ability to steer your enterprise.

Abiding by Corporation Securities Laws

Securities laws are meant to protect investors from unscrupulous business owners. These laws require corporations to jump through some hoops before accepting investments in exchange for shares of stock (the "securities"). Technically, a corporation is required to register the sale of shares with the federal Securities and Exchange Commission (SEC) and its state securities agency before granting stock to the initial corporate owners (shareholders). Registration takes time and typically involves extra legal and accounting fees. For more information on SEC rules regarding stock sales, see Chapter 9.

Fortunately, many small corporations get to skip the registration process because of exemptions provided by both federal and state laws. For example, SEC rules don't require a corporation to register a "private offering," which is a nonadvertised sale of stock to either:

- a limited number of people (generally 35 or fewer), or
- those who, because of their net worth or income earning capacity, can reasonably be expected to take care of themselves in the investment process.

Most states have enacted their own versions of this popular federal exemption.

If you and a few associates are setting up a corporation that you'll actively manage, you will no doubt qualify for an exemption, and you will not have to file any paperwork. For more information about federal exemptions, visit the SEC website (www.sec.gov). For more information on your state's exemption rules, go to your secretary of state's website.

Summary of Loans vs. Investments		
Source	Loans	Investment
Advantages	The lender has no management say or direct entitlement to profits in your business.	Investors are sometimes partners or board members and often offer valuable advice and assistance.
	Your only obligation to the lender is to repay the loan on time. Loans from close relatives can have flexible repayments terms.	You can be flexible about repayment requirements.
	Interest payments (but not principal payments) are a deductible business expense.	If your business loses money or goes broke, you won't have personal liability—that is, you won't have to repay your investors.
Disadvantages	You may have to make loan repayments when your need for cash is greatest, such as during your business's startup or expansion.	Equity investors dilute your ownership and require a greater share of your profits than interest on a loan.
	You may have to assign a security interest in your property to obtain a loan, which may place your personal assets at risk.	Your investors must be informed about all significant business events and can influence or dominate management.
	Under most circumstances, you can be sued personally for any unpaid balance of the loan, even if it's unsecured.	Your investors can sue you if they feel their rights are being compromised.

Chapter 6

Communicating Your Ideas

The key to financing is communication. People who lend or invest in a business rely on what you say and how you say it before opening their checkbooks. You will have a difficult time convincing people to give up their money for your ideas if your communications fail to meet professional standards.

This chapter provides an introduction to several types of communication: phone calls, letters, presentations, your business proposal, and your business plan. Each of these serves a distinct purpose and has a distinct format, though you will find there is substantial room for you to improvise. Chapter 7 provides more detail on your business proposal and explains the principles in a typical business plan.

The Hidden Message

If the ultimate purpose of your communication is to acquire financing or a licensing deal, then you must take the viewpoint of the potential investor, lender, or licensee and structure your writing accordingly. People who invest or loan money are concerned about your success. Investors, for example, want a venture that will earn extraordinary profit from growth, not ongoing income. (There are rare exceptions to these rules—for example, friends or relatives who want to support you without losing a lot of money.)

From the point of view of people with money (investors, lenders, and licensees), the quest for a substantial profit is tempered by the fact that, according to the Small Business Administration, fifty percent of startups fail in the first year. About one-third of these failures result in a complete loss of the money invested (perhaps even more if lawsuits are involved). Investors are aware of these risks and will endeavor—using business smarts and documentation—to avoid it.

So how do you communicate the information that will convince a practical business person that not only won't your business be in the 50% that fail, but that it will be in the two or three percent that have great success? In other words, how do you structure your letters and business proposal so that you present an attractive, profitable opportunity?

The most effective and time-tested formula for writing successful communication is the one used by advertising writers and known by the acronym AIDA:

- attract **A**ttention
- arouse **I**nterest
- create **D**esire
- ask for **A**ction

Obviously, not every letter, email, or phone conversation needs to include these elements. But if you can incorporate these elements into crucial communications, you will gradually attract and keep the attention of your prospective money source. Any communication that poses as "important" but is not will appear as an intrusion on the recipient's time and as an unwelcome distraction. Think of all of the junk mail you get daily, and how fast much of it goes into the trash—some of it not even opened.

Image your communication a little bit like the story of the man and his horse. Consider this old tale: A man was crossing the plains with his horse. When night came, he set up his tent and was about to go to sleep. His horse called to him and asked if it might put just its feet in through the flap of the tent because it was so very cold. The man agreed that just the feet would be acceptable. As the night went on, the horse asked if it might put its legs in, and the man acceded. Soon the horse was inside the tent, and the man was outside. If the horse had asked if it could come into the tent all at once, the answer would have been a resounding no, of course. We must enter our prospect's tent a toe at a time.

Start any important communication with the idea that your statement and tone must create sufficient interest so that the reader wants to proceed. The interest must be built and sustained.

Don't diminish the dignity of your communication by bragging how great your invention is and how it will create enormous profits. Such tactics may work well for the automobile dealer whose TV commercial is in the decibel range of a jet aircraft during takeoff, but they are seldom well received when appealing to a sophisticated investor.

Profit must always be suggested subtly. Persons who have made substantial money in their own business are less susceptible to claims of "my invention is great, and will make you millions." Your focus should be on two main points:

- The proprietary advantage of your invention or great idea (the patent, exclusive distribution, and so forth).
- The new customers to be gained through the introduction of your invention to a market that already awaits it.

These speak to the essence of entrepreneurship rather than scream dollar signs at the reader. The ideal response to any important communication is to get to the next step—for example, a personal meeting at which you will demonstrate your prototype and discuss the amount of money you are seeking.

Telephone Calls

Soliciting a lender, investor, or licensee by phone is a difficult, if not impossible, task. To initiate this type of arrangement, you will need a sales mentality. The task is to reach the right person and, in a very short time, convince that person that you have something worth their time (and investment).

Keep in mind that each person in the line to the decision maker is important and that you may need to befriend everyone, including the receptionist. Therefore, it is foolish ever to speak curtly or act rudely. How do you reach the

Should You Call First or Send a Proposal?

Andy Gibbs, the CEO of Patent Café, and I have a friendly disagreement about how to contact prospective angels. Andy says to phone them directly—don't contact them initially with a letter. There is no question that the most powerful selling is done face to face or over the phone using the business proposal as a script, rather than mailing it to an angel. A phone call enables you to confront objections head on and diplomatically guide the conversation. However, it is my observation that few inventors have the sales temperament or the practice for the direct approach. If you phone, your prospect will ask the nature of your product, and you must attempt to sell it without the benefit of being able to edit what you have said, and polish and restate it as you have done in your business proposal. As Joanne Hayes-Rines, the publisher of *Inventors' Digest* always says, you only have one chance to create a first impression. Thus, I maintain that most inventors (though not all) shouldn't risk the initial contact by telephone and should send the proposal, instead. This is a decision only you can make.

right person? In subsequent chapters I help you identify the types of individuals who make funding decisions: licensees, strategic and investment partners, and institutional lenders.

In the event you must leave a phone message, here a few suggestions. Have your major credibility points written down and handy during your call. For example, you 1) are an inventor with two patents and a graduate of Pratt Institute; 2) are knowledgeable about the market for products such as Product X and Y; and 3) have a patent pending on a device that is more cost-efficient than the present devices. Having a list of points to cover will help prevent you from forgetting them if you're nervous or flustered.

Whenever you speak with someone (not voice mail), follow the same approach and also:

- Get the name of the person—always keep a record of every person you speak with.
- Keep the conversation short—don't get sidetracked. You should be friendly, but remember, the person on the phone is at work and your call is the equivalent to a sales pitch.
- Get a direct mailing address—you want to follow up the call with a letter.
- Stick to the facts, and stick to the truth—don't deceive the caller in the hopes of making a sale. Any

pitch that is based upon deceptions will eventually fall apart.

- Thank the person at the end of the call and indicate how you intend to follow-up.

It may seem obvious to most people, but it's also worth remembering that it's not a good idea to make important calls on a cell phone if there is a likelihood that reception will be weak or the call may be cut off.

Letters and Email

Letters and emails should be brief, professional, and to the point. With today's modern word processing, there is no excuse for producing unprofessional correspondence or letters that have grammatical or spelling errors. Use templates to create your stationery (supplied with all word processing programs), and always run spelling and grammar checkers before sending any letter (no matter how short the correspondence). You may think there are no typos in your letter, but you'll always be amazed what spell checkers turn up. Also, it may seem obvious, but keep copies of all correspondence (including copies of email).

If possible, keep your sentences short. If you are writing a cover letter (a letter to introduce another document), write in a manner that will attract attention to and arouse interest in that document. To gain your recipient's attention and

arouse his or her interest, it sometimes helps to establish your credibility.

Here's an example of sample solicitation letter by an inventor seeking a licensee.

January 10, 2005

Re: New Innovation—Improved
 Soft Drink Packaging

Dear Ms. Walters:

I'm a graduate of Cooper Union with considerable experience in the field of packaging and design. Several years ago, I began researching a better method of mass market packaging cases of canned soft drinks. Last year, I reduced to practice a novel method that could be less expensive than your present method and can better protect your products. I am presently applying for patent protection for this process. I would very much like to discuss this innovation with you as I believe [*name of company*] would find it to be a valuable method of preserving your product and reducing costs. I look forward to speaking with you.

Sincerely,

Edward James

Edward James

Product Presentations

It's likely that as part of any financing decision, the investor or lender will want a presentation of your great idea. A presentation is one of the most important forms of communication. Here are some suggestions:

- **Be clear, fast, and concise.** This is a sales pitch, not a dissertation. Hit the high points (cost, effectiveness, product superiority, and so forth) quickly.
- **Practice your presentation, but don't memorize or read it.** Your talk should have a conversational quality, which is most likely to engage your listeners.
- **Know your costs.** The "financials" will probably be the first area of concern for a potential licensee. What will it cost to manufacture and sell your invention? How much can be earned? Have your business proposal on hand.
- **Stick to the facts; stick to business.** It's fine to be friendly, but focus on the purpose of your visit, which is to convince people at the meeting to invest in or license your invention.
- **Be prepared.** Give your presentation a trial run. If you will need electrical power or additional facilities, even just a desk or bulletin board, make sure you will have them. Every marketer has disaster stories about prototypes that failed or facilities that were unsuitable for presentation. Have a contingency plan. For example, "I'm afraid my power supply has died. In any event, I have a video that shows how this device functions, and I'd be happy to leave it with you so you can see a demonstration."
- **Be flexible.** Be open to ideas and suggested modifications that are offered. Always "take them under advisement," although you probably shouldn't make changes until you can determine the seriousness of the investor's or licensee's commitment.
- **Be positive, without being manically upbeat.** Nobody wants to hear from a sad sack. Walk a line between enthusiasm for your invention and a calm business demeanor.
- **Have written materials to supplement your demonstration.** Use simple written materials such as numbered lists of your product's strengths to make your point. Determine the right moment to hand out paperwork—before, during, or after a presentation. Charts, graphs, and tables have a powerful effect in presentations and can make your point better than a spreadsheet.
- **Get feedback.** Ask for opinions. Even if the current audience is not interested, they may have suggestions that can benefit you in your next presentation.
- **Don't take it personally.** Don't appear offended by rejection.

You should never have to accept someone else's bad manners, but don't confuse rudeness with simple rejection. If you want to stay in the invention business, you may have to deal with the same people over and over. Curb your anger and resentment, as they will be interpreted as a sign of unprofessionalism and may affect your ability to license in the future.

Personal Appearance Counts

Unlike letters and phone calls, an in-person solicitation may be affected by your appearance. Your grooming, clothes, and personal hygiene should demonstrate that you are a credible business person. You should have business cards available, and you should obtain a business card from any individual that you speak with. And, as with phone conversations, keep the discussion short and stick to the facts.

Business Proposal

Think of your business proposal like a resume for your invention business. It explains why your invention is a great idea, why it's needed, why your solution is the right one, what the competition is like, and how your product will stand out and create extraordinary profits. I explain how to draft a business proposal and provide an example in Chapter 7.

Business Plan

The business plan is a document that describes and analyzes your business and provides a method of forecasting the business's future. It is a document that is sometimes needed by entrepreneurial inventors. It is rarely needed by the inventor-for royalties.

Business plans come in many forms. All follow proscribed rules, share certain qualities, and have certain functions, but some are more formal than others. Every plan includes an Introduction/ Summary (sometimes called an Executive Summary) that summarizes the plan; this section is often the focus of lenders and investors. (The plan summary incorporates much of your business proposal, discussed above.) Every plan also includes a description of the business and its accomplishments, as well as a sales forecast, a profit and loss forecast, a cash flow forecast, and a spending plan.

Business plans usually run 30 to 50 pages and require considerable work to prepare and polish. Most independent investors (what I refer to as "angels") don't initially want a formal business plan, and submitting one may be counterproductive. There's too much reading.

That's why I recommend using a business proposal at first. More information on drafting a business plan is provided in Chapter 7.

Preparing Your Business Proposal or Business Plan

In his book *Burn Your Business Plan!: What Investors Really Want From Entrepreneurs* (Lauson Publishing), author David Gumpert argues that even when investors ask for a business plan, they really don't want one. He backs this up with studies and surveys that demonstrate that business plans are often more of a hindrance than an asset when seeking investment. They're too long, contain technical mumbo-jumbo, and often have crazy projections and inappropriate management information. Gumpert is in favor of summarizing information, particularly financials, and presenting that information in a succinct, direct manner. Gumpert states, "Entrepreneurs have increasingly made the business plan an end in itself, and all the while investors have increasingly come to view the business plan as merely one element of a much larger process."

A business plan may be necessary in some situations (and Gumpert acknowledges this), and later in this chapter, I discuss the basics of preparing one. But for the most part, you will have a better chance finding and convincing many an investor by emphasizing key business points in a succinct document.

Your business proposal covers how the invention is protected; explains its commercial potential; and describes how participants will become shareholders in a small, but formally organized, company, and how that company plans to earn a significant profit. By preparing it, you familiarize yourself with the salient business qualities of your invention so that you don't approach prospective partners with a "half-baked" concept. In short, it's a powerful, versatile tool. Think of it as your company's resume.

Always suggest that potential investors check with their own financial and legal advisers to evaluate the investment. Although each investor will assess his or her own degree of risk, you should disclose all the relevant information to them so they can make an intelligent, informed choice.

Two Sample Summaries

Rather than describe what's required, let's first take a look at two business proposals, one for an office product and another for a device for dispensing gasoline. The first invention that is the subject of this business proposal is one of the many "great ideas" I get from time to time, and abandon. So, pay attention to the format and the objectives of the writing, not the imaginary prospects of my "throw-away" invention.

Business Proposal for an Innovative Office Product

The Market Need

Nearly all office files today use suspended pockets such as Pendaflex® brand. The pockets are hung in metal frames that consist of side bars and front and rear brackets. Because some file cabinets are longer from front to back, the side bars are produced to accommodate the longest files. This necessitates cutting off a few inches from the bars in order to fit the most popular size of files. Presently, the only practical way to cut these heavy bars is with a hacksaw—a tool that typically is not found in offices.

Innovative Office Products, Inc., a startup corporation, has developed and patented a shear that trims the extra length from the side bars. This shear is foot operated, is easy to use, and is safe. The operator places the bar in the shear and steps on the pedal, and, in less than five seconds total, the bar is ready for assembly. (The hacksawing method takes at least two minutes per bar and can cause injuries.)

More important than time saved is the convenience. Sawing the bars creates metal particles that embed in the carpet or scratch a tile floor. And many a desk has been marred by using it as a workbench during sawing.

The Market

Every office in every country that uses suspended files is a potential customer. Even that rare office that has a hacksaw tucked away in a desk drawer will immediately recognize the advantages of our shear invention.

Profitability

Our shear is manufactured from high-volume, low-cost methods. We anticipate low manufacturing costs and exceptional markup due to the customer's perception of its value. Sales volume through retail outlets such as Office Max, Office Depot, and Staples will be high. Our patent will preclude immediate competition. And our ground-floor position with the office supply super markets (which will want only one source) will foreclose competition. Thus, we anticipate early positive cash flow and rapid growth.

Ultimate Disposition

After sales volume grows to a highly profitable level, our goal is to sell to, or merge the company with, a manufacturer of a line of office equipment such as staplers, hole punchers, or paper cutters.

Our Need

We offer a significant portion of our treasure stock in exchange for a cash investment of $75,000. We welcome an investor who will act as a mentor and optionally as an active partner.

For More Information, and to Arrange a Meeting

Please contact us by phone or by returning the postcard included with this letter. Thank you.

Innovative Office Products, Inc.
P.O. Box 4321
Old Town, California 93342
Phone 1-800-555-1234

Business Proposal for a Safe Gasoline Dispensing Accessory

The Market Need

The average homeowner today typically has two containers of gasoline in his garage or garden shed: one for straight gas, and the other for a gas/oil mixture. Pouring gas from the container into the gas tank is not only inconvenient, but it is hazardous. The marketing opportunity is for a spout that replaces the typical flexible hose that comes with the gas container and offers semiautomatic valving and one-hand operation.

The Market

There are approximately 35 million homes in the U. S., and most of these have lawns that require cutting. Nearly all lawns are cut with a gasoline-motorized lawnmower. Nearly all of these lawnmowers use straight gasoline. Most of these homes use weed cutters of some type, and these typically use the gas/oil mix. The majority of these homes are in cooler climates, and snow blowers use either straight gas or a gas/oil mix. The theoretical maximum market potential, therefore, is for 70 million units. Assuming that merely 10 percent of homeowners will eventually purchase my invention, priced at $3.95, the market potential is $27.65 million. With this kind of safety and convenience item, and the publicity it will generate, we expect a break-even point within the first three years. The potential of $27.65 million should be reached within five years. Thus, average annual sales are just over $5 million. Assuming that we are too optimistic by a factor of three, annual sales of $1.7 million can be expected. Annual sales should maintain or climb gradually but continually after the 10 percent level is reached.

Profitability

Our device has been reviewed by two seasoned product designers, and CAD drawings of the components have been quoted by manufacturers and job shops over a range of 10,000 to 100,000 per order. The main components of our device are plastic injection molded. One component is a wire-form. Minor components (a hinge pin and a gasket) are less than five percent of total cost. Our projected offshore manufacturing costs are $.70 to $.76 including all labor and packaging. At a selling price of $3.95, our sale price-to-cost of manufacture ranges from 5.2 to 5.6. The device is in "patent applied for" status, and judging by the results of our patent search, we expect to be granted a strong patent.

Ultimate Disposition

Initially, we will orchestrate the logistics and use a fulfillment service to process orders. Overhead will be limited to a home office. There will be no salaries, although profit will be drawn by the inventor per advance written agreement with investors. Sometime between the fifth and sixth year, with sales still climbing and profits increasing, we expect to sell the product line assets, including tooling and the intellectual property, to a manufacturer of gasoline containers. If such manufacturers are not interested, we will search for a manufacturer of similar items or complementary products.

Our Need

We offer a significant portion of our stock in exchange for a cash investment of $98,000, about three-quarters of which will be used to purchase tooling, and the remainder will be used for penetrating marketing channels.

For more information, and to arrange a meeting

Please contact us by phone, or email, or by returning the postcard included herewith. Thank you.

Ivan Darenkovitch, LLC
P.O. Box 46
Springfield, Connecticut
Phone: 203-555-3418
Email: ivan@darenkovitchllc.com

Drafting Your Business Proposal

The structure of the business proposal is not sacred, but you must include certain expected information in order to trigger the desired response. Moreover, every page must carry the theme that your new product will have a receptive market and will produce a profit. Always keep in mind that the proposal is a carefully crafted advertisement of your invention product.

Succinctly Describe Your Invention and Its Prospects

Be aware that your reader isn't interested in a heroic saga at this point, so avoid the temptation to tell a story of your new product's conception and development. Later, after you have received the loan or investment, you can tell your story if you feel that you must. In your business proposal you should focus on three key points:

- Why your new product is needed (what problem it solves, how it benefits the customer, and so forth), and the fact that it has a waiting market.
- Why your product is the right one from the user's perspective (it is easy to use, saves time, saves money, improves efficiency, and so forth.).

- Why your product will produce extraordinary profit—for example, it's proprietary and inexpensive to produce. If you are offering a "me, too" product—merely another way to accomplish what other products already accomplish—you will have a difficult time establishing this point.

All other points are subordinate to these three. Your physical description, the drawings and photographs, the patents, and other documentation only support these three key points.

Keep in mind that providing a prospectus (and following SEC prospectus rules) is required when you do not qualify for a stock offering exemption—for example, you are soliciting more than 35 investors. For more on stock offering exemptions, see Chapter 9. You may be tempted to tell more of your story in order to sell your potential investor on your invention or great idea. But too much detail is counterproductive and is best left to a meeting where you can sense the investor's position and respond flexibly. The main purpose of the business proposal is to create the desire for a meeting, not the immediate desire to invest. Remember, your business proposal must tell why your product is needed, why your solution for this need is the right one, and why your product will produce extraordinary profit.

What's a Stock Prospectus?

I modeled the business proposal after some of the elements of a typical stock prospectus. Although it is not intended to function as a prospectus (and you shouldn't label it as such to investors), your summary does borrow its presentation from this formal document. In case you've never seen one, a prospectus contains:

- the objective of the investment
- the company's financial condition
- how investors' money will be used
- risks of ownership
- expenses and management fees

The Securities and Exchange Commission (SEC) requires a stock prospectus to ensure that investors are fully informed regarding publicly offered investments. A prospectus must be approved by the agency. If you're not familiar with the format, you should examine a few—found in most business books or online. Most investment or brokerage sites online can link you to various companies or mutual fund prospectuses.

Keep in mind that providing a prospectus (and following SEC prospectus rules) is required when you do not qualify for a stock offering exemption—for example, you are soliciting more than 35 investors. For more on stock offering exemptions, see Chapter 9.

What Your Business Proposal *Doesn't* Need to Include

Here are some questions that you *don't* need to address in your proposal.

- **Why will it succeed?** This is not the first question on the angel's mind. Angels want growth. A "small potatoes" business that succeeds and earns a decent living for an entrepreneur will be of no interest to an angel if it will not grow rapidly into a size that is attractive to a larger corporation, investment group, or venture capitalist.

- **What do you want to start or change?** A fair question. But your business proposal is based on an invention or great idea, not a traditional business. You must emphasize the invention, not the kind of business that you anticipate as the vehicle for profiting from your invention.

- **How much money is required?** Ideally, you would like to postpone this question until you have a face-to-face meeting, unless you have prepared a very thorough budget of expenses and you are sure of

How I Discovered the Value of Business Proposals

Several years ago I owned a small manufacturing business. When it came time to sell my business and move on to other challenges, I took the conventional route. I placed an ad in the *Los Angeles Times*. I had 15 or so responses, as I recall, and four of these advanced to the stage of a personal meeting. Each of these persons occupied me for at least three or four hours as I toured them through my facility and showed them the books. It wasn't surprising that none of them made an offer; selling a business is not an easy thing to do.

As I contemplated my next ad, I dreaded the inevitable distractions to come. Then, it occurred to me that I could avoid most of these "time sinks" by preparing a written document that covered all of the FAQs (frequently asked questions). I remembered receiving such a document that was trying to get me to invest in a certain stock. And so I wrote a business proposal for my business and offered it in my ad, which read as follows:

For sale: Precision sheet-metal manufacturing business. Phone for business proposal. 714-555-1234.

I received 26 phone calls. A few callers asked for details on the phone, but I politely steered them to the business proposal. As a result of my business proposals I met face to face with only two of the 26 people, and one bought the business. One caller was a business broker. After reading my business proposal he phoned just to tell me that he thought my approach was excellent. I've been an incurable business proposal user ever since.

Now, you may have picked up on the significant increase in response I received when I offered the business proposal, as against presenting only my phone number. Apparently most people are reluctant to engage in conversation for fear of sales pressure, wasted time, and so on. But when one can deal impersonally—at a safe distance, we might say—using the business proposal as a tool, then the prospective financier retains a comfortable level of control. The number of face-to-face contacts goes down, and the quality of the responses goes up.

The moral of this story applies directly to the financing of your invention: Deal with quantity, and manage that quantity with your business proposal. Not only will you wear yourself out if you try to make all contacts in person, but the number of contacts you must make in order to conclude a financial agreement are often so many that you will likely give up before finding the right prospect. Think on this: Several million human sperm start their journey.

How I Discovered the Value of Business Proposals (continued)

Roughly 200 make it to their destination, and one penetrates the egg. But penetration only happens about one-fourth of the time. Nature understands the need for quantity. So, too, in the approach to getting an angel to invest we must resort to quantity, knowing well that most of our business proposal packages will fall on impenetrable ground. But don't be discouraged. There are many reasons why the seem-ingly perfect candidates for your invention won't be interested in financing it, and these reasons may have little or nothing to do with the merits of your invention itself. Often an angel is fully subscribed and has no more time or money to invest. Sometimes the angel just won't warm up to your kind of invention. And sometime the angel simply won't want to drive 50 miles to work with you.

how much money you will need. If you do state the amount you need, place it near the end of the business proposal, but leave the amount of stock you will yield in exchange for the face-to-face meeting.

- **What's the return on investment?** At the startup phase, you have no way to estimate this. Even if you did, it likely would not agree with what your angel has in mind. And the risk of startups is high. An estimate of ROI at this time is premature.
- **Why is the venture a good risk?** It isn't. It's only a fair risk. Your angel knows that. To present your venture as having low risk will suggest self-deception and naiveté to the angel.

Keep It Short and Looking Sharp

Let's discuss the ideal length of your business proposal. We can take clues from two sources: the publishing business (books are inventions, too), and business plans that are effective.

Publishers and their agents who are receptive to proposals from authors generally ask for a one-page or (at most) two-page synopsis or outline of the work. And executive summaries found in books and guides on business plans usually are one or two pages. One or two pages should be sufficient to get across the essence of the three key points mentioned in the previous chapter. But if your business proposal is well written, it won't be thrown away if it has three pages, especially if it is visually attractive.

A "designed page"—one that leaves plenty of white space, avoids long paragraphs, and uses a traditional type font and size—is inviting and readable. A crowded page, one with less than inch-and-a-quarter margins and long paragraphs without headings, is uninviting. The recipient will dread reading such a document. This is not the fine print on the back of your insurance policy that you are writing. It is a sales document. The reader must sense organization, neatness, and an immediate verbal appeal to his or her interests.

Don't Estimate Manufacturing Costs

You may be tempted to go into detail concerning the cost of manufacture. My advice at this point is that, unless you are a manufacturing expert and have solicited several price quotes from the most appropriate vendors, stick to generalities. A statement such as, "Our shear product lends itself to low-cost manufacture from stamped steel and molded plastic" is sufficient. It may be risky or misleading to list specific cost figures, since few inventors have the expertise or time to seek out the latest and greatest manufacturing processes and sources of subcontracting. Keep in mind that an inventor's conjecture about costs is often too high.

Of course, if you have the money to hire an experienced product designer—

one who is an expert in manufacturing processes as well as design—then have this person produce manufacturing drawings, and use these to solicit price quotations for each component. Then, and only then, will you be in a position to speak with authority about the probable cost of your product.

Keep in mind that even if you have component manufacturing costs, you may not forecast accurately, since manufacturing costs depend heavily on a prediction of sales volume. In order to speak with convincing authority, you must prepare costs at various sales volumes.

EXAMPLE: Let's say that one key component in your product will be injection-molded from plastic. The machine cycle time for injection molding is substantially the same whether your mold has one cavity, two, four, and so on. If the injection, cooling, and ejection cycle is half a minute, and the machine time costs $1.50 a minute, the cycle time will cost 75 cents. If your mold has a single cavity, each part will cost 75 cents plus the cost of the raw plastic. If your mold has four cavities, the machine cycle time cost per piece drops to less than 19 cents plus the cost of the raw plastic. (75 cents divided by the number of cavities.) "Cavity" is simply the name for the shaped volume into which the plastic is injected to form your part.

Ah, you say, I'll base my costs on a 16-cavity mold. Hold on! A 4-cavity mold may cost you $25,000, and a 16-cavity mold may cost you $60,000. (These are hypothetical costs, but not unrealistic.) If you plan to sell a million units, obviously you will need a mold with some large number of cavities, perhaps 16. But if your volume is small, you will probably find that paying off a 16-cavity mold from the savings in unit cost will take ten years. And your product may be obsolete in five years—or even less.

As your forecast of sales increases, more elaborate tooling or processing reduces cost per unit, but, at the same time, you must pay more for that tooling. Therefore, as I suggested, it is dangerous to predict costs unless you do so with respect to a forecast of sales volume and you understand manufacturing.

Some inventors take a two-step approach, first seeking a small investment to cover designing and preparing manufacturing drawings, then a larger investment to pay for production tooling and market introduction later if the estimated profit margin is attractive. This is not the best way to approach a potential investor, but if you can't afford these preparation costs any other way, you might still get money if your product is sufficiently attractive.

⚠ Don't distribute your business proposal to the public. In subsequent chapters we'll discuss to whom to send your business proposal but as general rule you should avoid any appearance of soliciting the general public, which can lead to violations of state and federal security laws. (See Chapter 9 for more on the SEC rules.) However, you should feel comfortable sending it to business people you already know. You don't have to know them intimately.

For example, when you go to the dentist, have a business proposal with you. During those rare intervals when your mouth isn't crowded with mirrors, drain tubes, and plaque scrapers, mention your company and its prospects for success based on an "innovative product." Avoid such words as "invention" or "inventor." Inventing may be of importance to us, but from the investor's perspective it is only one among many ways to earn a substantial return on his or her investment.

After You Send Your Business Proposal

A well-written business proposal, mailed with a convenient reply card included, will make your campaign efficient both in time saved and results obtained. Just don't hope to connect by sending out five or ten business proposals to seemingly "sure thing" candidates. More

Post Card

Does a post card seem too informal for such important communication? It isn't. Time after time I have used this approach in various matters, always with good results.

One of my early ventures was a survey of building contractors to determine their satisfaction with nail guns. More than half of my post cards came back, and several of them had hand-written comments that were very informative.

Another time I used this approach in helping a friend with her job search. She mailed out 25 unsolicited resumes and received 17 post card replies! Two of these checked the "Call me for an interview" check box. And she was hired. At the time this was entirely unorthodox as a way to receive response from prospective employers. But whether prospective employer or prospective investor, people appreciate this little courtesy and convenience.

The post card with appropriate check boxes is nonthreatening, is easy to use, and offers a refreshing, innovative means of responding quickly. If the response is to be rejection, the recipient may delay a written letter. You don't want to invite rejection, of course. But if the response is to be a definite no, you want to hear this in a week, not in six months or never.

Here are some of the check boxes that you may want on your post card:

☐ Please phone me for an appointment.
☐ I'm pressed for time right now, but I'll get back to you around _____ .
☐ No interest here at this time. I suggest you send a business proposal to:
☐ No interest here at this time.

Comments/name/phone number:

_____

_____

The standard-size post card may be a bit crowded for the responses you wish to list, especially if you want to provide a generous space for comments. The maximum "legal" post card size for regular postcard postage is 4¼ by 6 inches. Anything larger than this requires a first-class stamp. Four pieces of size 4¼ by 5½ inches can be cut from a standard sheet of card stock, which is available from your local office-supply store. The largest-sized post card that can be mailed for the full first-class stamp is 6⅛ by 11½ inches.

Be sure that you include at least the name of the company in the "return address" position on the post card. I once neglected this and got back a post card that wanted more information, and I hadn't a clue as to where to send it. And don't forget to print your own address on the front of the card.

likely at least ten times those numbers will be needed to get even a few positive responses.

No News Is No News

There is an old saying that no news is good news. Maybe. But being ignored for more than a few weeks is just plain bad manners on the part of the recipient. Even when the answer is, "We aren't ready to give you an answer yet," that answer is a reasonable response. If you are ignored, you have the right to phone the recipient and ask the status of his or her response. There is a time to approach people with humility, but this isn't it.

If you are dealing with a company, you may get the "Mrs. Smith is in a meeting" routine. Pin down her gatekeeper to a time when she can be reached. If you still get the run-around after three calls, ask the gatekeeper to find your reply card and mail it back. This will usually work because the gatekeeper (administrative assistant, whatever) knows that you can get through to her and won't want the embarrassment and annoyance of more calls from you.

Face-to-Face Meetings

When you meet with a prospective investor, you should present your case in a structured, well-rehearsed manner. As inventors, we will want to talk about our invention, of course. But your invention, or mine, is not what primarily interests any prospective source of finance; it is the promise of extraordinary profits (thus growth) earned from a venture that has challenge and excitement.

Always sell the benefits of your invention, not the invention itself. And sell the benefits of working with you and your startup. You can perfect your sales pitch for money by spending days writing it and rewriting it until you talk in your sleep about it. You can critique it and reshape it until you have a convincing sales tool. But if you speak extemporaneously—without a script, either written or memorized—you are far less likely to control your presentation and say the right things in the right order.

Studies have shown that when a prospect is given visual information along with the same spoken information, the impact is significantly increased. This is why slides with text are projected in well-organized seminars and other presentations. Visual information can be highlighted with color or italics or text boxes. But, more important, it presents the sales pitch in a sequence that follows proven principles of how to convince people using words.

Also, keep in mind that every invention has an interesting story—interesting to the inventor and his family maybe, but not necessarily interesting to the person from whom you hope to extract money. At some point in discussion, after the structured presentation, when you are on your feet walking out of the confer-ence room, you may slip in your story if asked. But if you have already made the sale, stop talking. Don't spoil things by sounding like an inventor.

Your Business Plan

As I explained earlier in this chapter, investors usually don't want full-blown business plans, and when they get them they rarely read through the 50+ pages of materials and statistics. Business plans are usually just too long and often have unrealistic projections. That said, you may be required to prepare a business plan for a specific investor or borrower, or you may have grown to the point where a full business plan is essential for projecting your future.

First impressions matter, and if your business plan does not look and read like other plans—that is, it doesn't in-clude the typical headings and subject matter—then a presumption is created in the reader's mind that something is lacking; or, to put it bluntly, that you are an unprofessional business person. At the same time, do not assume that you can copy the headings and substantial language from someone else's plan and create the "illusion" of a professional plan. If you're going to do a business plan, do it right.

The easiest way to do it right is to use one of the business plan creation tools. I recommend two in particular—the

publishers of both offer a money-back guarantee.

- *How to Write a Business Plan,* by Mike McKeever (Nolo). (Cost approximately $24) This popular book is one of the most comprehen-sive guides to creating a business plan, and it can help to evaluate profitability; estimate operating expenses; prepare cash flow; create profit and loss forecasts; determine assets; liabilities; and net worth; find potential sources of financing (up-to-date sources are provided); and learn how to present your plan to lenders and investors. The book in-cludes a CD-ROM with spreadsheets that help you determine and fore-cast cash flow, financial statements, sales revenue, and profit and loss.

- *Business Plan Pro,* (Palo Alto Software) (Cost approximately $79) is consistently ranked as the best plan-creation software, and for good reason. It contains more than four hundred sample business plans and provides a question-and-answer format to get you going. You can estimate your numbers, and the program's preformatted tables build your financial statements for you, then check your financials for accuracy. Other helpful features are templates that allow you to present your plan via PowerPoint and a Venture Capital Database that provides you with an easy way to find potential investors (over 1,200 venture capital firms are listed). The book *Hurdle: The Book on Business Planning,* by Tim Berry, is also included.

Although I cannot explain how to write a business plan—I'd rather leave that to the experts—I can offer you a few suggestions when you are preparing your own:

- You may be tempted to begin by writing the introduction (sometimes referred to as the "executive summary"). Don't. Prepare the rest of the plan, first, then come back to do the introduction/summary. An introduction/summary is best abstracted from the written full plan, and the full plan should proceed from an outline.

- Always write from the reader's perspective—that is, considering the investor's or lender's objectives. Your mission and opportunity is to create a dream that can be realistically achieved and support it with enough facts and logic so that your reader will read on.

- When discussing your market opportunity, you must have at least one substantial proprietary advantage. If your product has no competition (many an inventor's dream), this may or may not be a market opportunity. It sounds great at first, but, if no one has yet filled the demand, possibly the demand is too small to justify market entry through traditional channels. Many products are sold via the Internet that can't be sold profitably through the formal channels.

- When discussing strategy, focus on how you will penetrate the market, and dominate it (or become a formidable number two).

- Many investors look first to the management team and second to the product in their selection process. At a minimum, you will have to have a strong full-time marketing person and an experienced full-time manager

Sample Business Plan

I've provided a sample business plan from an invention company that has two patented products. This sample plan—which is several years old—was written by Larry Healy and is excerpted from *How to Write a Business Plan,* by Mike McKeever (Nolo).

DAY INTERNATIONAL, INC.

AN INVESTMENT OPPORTUNITY

April 16, 2005

DAY INTERNATIONAL, INC. • 123 Smith Place • San Jose, CA
Telephone (408) 555-1212

Table of Contents

A. Introduction

After several years of development work, DAY INTERNATIONAL, INC. is ready to market two unique electronic devices, both of which use the same patented new technology. This technology utilizes computerized optic displays to create a programmable message. In commercial application, this is valuable in creating commercial signs and displays which use a scrolling technique to attract and inform customers. As a recreational product, computerized optical displays using this technology can be made to respond directly to music and voice patterns. In other words, full color visual displays result from sound. This product application is particularly attractive to young people.

Extensive market research suggests a large market for both the commercial (Kinet-O-Scroll) and the recreational (Kinet-O-Scope) applications of this product. The commercial programmable sign market already exceeds one million dollars in the United States and is sure to grow quickly. Many units are purchased by retailers for what amounts to instant in-store advertising. In this application, the retailer can program a sign with information on that day's specials, and, presto, he has created his own attractive electronic display. The product, which is described more fully in the accompanying Product Description, below, has several features not now commercially available, including a wide choice of type styles. It will also have a substantial price advantage over other products now on the market. The consumer recreational market for this product is not fully tested, but there are a number of exciting potential uses.

DAY INTERNATIONAL, INC. is incorporated under the laws of the state of California and is ready to begin operations. The founders have spent several years of hard work preparing for this time and have made substantial personal investments. They are eager to proceed. However, because their personal financial resources are not adequate to manufacture and distribute sufficient units, they are prepared to offer a

1

one-third share of the corporation for an equity investment of $75,000. The enclosed financial projections demonstrate that if projections are met, there will be a very profitable return for the investor.

B. Company Description

DAY INTERNATIONAL, INC. was incorporated in California on June 1, 20__ as an outgrowth of Day Kinetics, a partnership formed in November of 19__. The corporation was organized to manufacture and sell several electronic display items for commercial and recreational purposes. The technology on which these products is based is covered by U.S. Patent (Smith #5676890123), for which an exclusive license has been obtained by the corporation. DAY INTERNATIONAL's offices are at 123 Smith Place, San Jose, CA, and the telephone number is (408) 555-1212. All stock is held by Frederick R. Jones and Phillip Court who, along with several family members, occupy seats on the Board of Directors.

Two seats on the Board of Directors are still to be filled. A minority shareholder, or shareholders who invest $75,000, will be permitted to seat two directors by majority vote. The majority shareholders are willing to prepare a formal shareholders' agreement, with the idea of protecting the interests of the minority shareholders.

C. Patent Status

Phillip Court, one of the directors and officers of DAY INTERNATIONAL, INC., obtained an exclusive license to the U.S. Patent on which the Kinet-O-Scroll and Kinet-O-Scope are based (Smith #5676890123) in 2002. This license was granted by the original inventor of the process, Elmo Smith, for 2% of any eventual sales of either product during the term of the patent, until Smith receives $200,000; 1.5% until Smith receives a total of $400,000; and 1% thereafter. This license is cancelable if Smith does not receive $20,000 per year with the first payment, due November 2003. The

2

license excludes certain applications of the Smith patent which are not related to the corporation's products.

In 2004, Phillip Court assigned an exclusive sublicense for the remaining term of the patent (10 years) to DAY INTERNATIONAL, INC. The payment to Court for this sublicense is 2% of the sales, expiring when sales of $100 million have been attained. In addition, the corporation has assumed the obligation for the royalty payment to Smith. All patent documentation, license agreements, and contracts are available to the potential investor or his agent upon request.

D. Corporation Management

The founders of DAY INTERNATIONAL, INC. are, Phillip V. Court and Frederick R. Jones, Jr.

The directors, officers, and key employees of this corporation are as follows:

1. Frederick R. Jones, Jr., President, Treasurer, and Director

2. Phillip V. Court, Vice-President, Secretary, and Director

3. Edmund R. Jones, Project Manager and Accounts Payable Manager.

Frederick R. Jones, Jr., age 52, has over 25 years of experience as an engineer, project engineer, program manager, proposal manager, marketing specialist, department head, program director, marketing manager, and so on. His specialty has been in automatic control systems and advanced display systems for manned aerospace vehicles. Mr. Jones's prior associations have been with Butterworth Aircraft (1974-1989), Vokar Electronics (1989-1999), and National Computer (1999 to date).

Phillip V. Court, age 46, has over 19 years of experience as an analog design engineer and manager. He is presently Engineering Manager of Data Conservation Products at a major corporation headquartered in

Santa Clara, California. Prior to this, he was the first vice-president of engineering of Ultradesign, a $200M sales semi-custom integrated circuit house. Mr. Court has authored numerous applications and brochures and several articles for a national electronics publication and holds three U.S. patents.

Edmund R. Jones, age 23, holds a Bachelor of Science degree in marketing from the University of California, Irvine. He has gained valuable work and customer interface experience at such companies as Reliable Insurance, VSV Associates and West Coast Semiconductor. In addition to his varied work experience, he has demonstrated community service and leadership capabilities, most significant of which are his leadership of a troop of explorer scouts and his membership in several regional opera societies. Edmund R. Jones is the son of Frederick R. Jones, Jr.

E. Product Description

The corporation plans to manufacture two products, both based on the Smith Patent. One of these is the Kinet-O-Scroll, which is designed for commercial applications. The other is the Kinet-O-Scope, which is designed for home recreational use. They are more fully described as follows.

The Kinet-O-Scroll: This consists of a scrolling "Times Square"-type message sign. Using its patented technology, DAY INTERNATIONAL, INC. can produce a moving sign that is more versatile, attractive, and economical than existing units. Basically, the Kinet-O-Scroll displays alphanumeric, graphic, and animated characters in full color. While the sign can be manufactured in numerous sizes, we plan to start with a unit with a screen measuring three feet vertically and four feet horizontally. All sorts of businesses, including restaurants, bars, banks, stores, real estate offices, airline terminals, bus stations, and so on, can use the Kinet-O-Scroll sign to inform customers of special events or offers at a comparatively low cost. The cost of the unit may further be reduced by users who make arrangements (tie-ins) for reimbursement by advertisers. This could be the case where companies that manufacture products or services that a retailer sells (for example, clothing, insurance, soft drinks) pay for advertising or provide their product at a better discount in exchange for advertising. There are hundreds of thousands of potential locations for such a low-cost merchandising tool.

The Kinet-O-Scroll is completely developed and tested. The first 100 production units have been completed, and a production capacity of over 200 units per month has been established. It is projected that the sales rate will rapidly build to a minimum of 100 units per month. This sales estimate, as well as long-term sales projections for the Kinet-O-Scroll, is based on extensive research into the need for this type of product, as well as into the sales history of existing (but inferior) products. This research has also involved consumer studies in which potential customers were asked to rate a variety of existing products against our new product.

In outline form, here is what we believe to be an objective summary of the "strip sign" market and the sales potential of the Kinet-O-Scroll:

- The Kinet-O-Scroll is unique in its mode of operation and its technical capacities. For example, it provides at least twice the visual resolution of other scrolling signs.

- There are at least a dozen manufacturers of programmable strip signs that can perform a somewhat similar but less-efficient function. The total annual sales of these products has been estimated (Advertising Graphics Magazine, Fall 1999) to be $10,000,000. This represents a 27% increase from last year.[1] The existent products are all very similar. No one manufacturer commands a dominant share of the market.

- The published prices of the strip signs that come the closest to having features similar to the Kinet-O-Scroll are in the $1,500 to

$2,000 range. As a result of efficiencies of design inherent in the patented technique used in the Kinet-O-Scroll, DAY's published list price is under $1,000.

- DAY's service contract (available on request) is above average for the industry.

- DAY's warranty policy (available on request) is above average for the industry.

The accompanying chart shows the sales volume of programmable signs in the United States in millions of dollars. In 2000, the total market for programmable signs is estimated to be $12,000,000. The corporation forecasts sales of 1,200 Kinet-O-Scroll units by the second year of production at a wholesale price of $550. These sales forecasts are considered conservative in that they are based on a market penetration of only five percent.

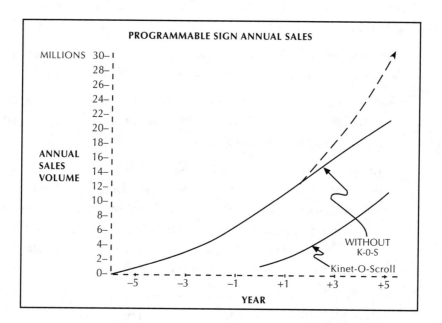

6

The Kinet-O-Scope: The Kinet-O-Scope features a small-sized screen which produces optic displays in response to the human voice, music, and other sounds. The display is in full color and the patterns created in response to sound are stunning. It is particularly attractive to young children experimenting with the sound of their own voice, although this is by no means the only market. People who love music, for example, are commonly fascinated by the Kinet-O-Scope. To accurately estimate the sales potential of the Kinet-O-Scope in the consumer market is difficult, as no directly comparable products exist.

In an effort to arrive at as accurate an estimate as possible, extensive consumer interviews were conducted. The Kinet-O-Scope Market Research Chart which follows summarizes the results of these interviews. When compared directly with the most similar products available (these are not nearly as good, but there is nothing else), 56% of the people asked preferred the Kinet-O-Scope. Even more persuasive, 49% of those tested would buy it for themselves, while 52% of those tested would buy it for a gift.

While there are no specific competitive products to the Kinet-O-Scope, it is clear that there is a distinct market for products of this type. This conclusion is arrived at by looking at good sales figures for Light Organs, Infinity Lights, Wave Devices, Volcano Lights, Rain Lamps, and other products which use light in innovative and creative ways.

Perhaps the best example of the size of the market is the Lava Light, a less technically advanced but lower-cost product. According to its manufacturer, Volcano Simplex International, over 6,000,000 units have been sold in four years, with 3,000,000 sold last year. If we consider a wholesale average selling price of $90, this represents over $270,000,000.

DAY INTERNATIONAL, INC. conservatively estimates that it will sell about 2,800 units of the Kinet-O-Scope in the second year of operations, for a wholesale dollar sales volume of $420,000 ($150 per unit). Further sales growth is expected in later years. Note that this unit volume is a tiny fraction of the Volcano Light's sales volume for last year.

Market Research

	Wave	Kinet-O-Scope	Rain Lamp	Light Organ	Lava Light	Infny Light
Preferred product	9%	56%	9%	1%	10%	13%
Already own it	2%	0%	2%	3%	4%	0%
Would buy it for self	32%	49%	18%	9%	16%	24%
Would buy it as gift	43%	52%	18%	11%	5%	31%
Estimated retail price	**	104.52	**	**	**	**
		105.54				
Notice of Avail		12%				
		5.3x				

Age: Under 16: 3%   16-20: 11%   21-34: 41%   35+: 45%

** Average Total Estimate: $168.69; Actual: $160.00

F. Marketing Plan

The channels of distribution for the Kinet-O-Scroll and Kinet-O-Scope will include direct sales by corporate personnel to selected major accounts and the use of manufacturer's representatives (sales reps), distributor's dealers (wholesalers), and international trading companies to reach the rest of the market. We do not anticipate establishing our own factory sales force. With regard to international sales, except for "opportunity sales," we will not launch our formal effort until we have adequately penetrated the domestic market. However, we will explore licensing our technology abroad.

In the beginning, DAY will team with a limited number of sales reps and wholesalers who have proven abilities in successfully introducing new

8

electronic products. At first, the emphasis will be on developing market penetration in a few carefully chosen regions near our manufacturing facility. The reason for this approach is to properly identify effective pricing techniques and marketing strategies. Information gathered will be used to fine-tune stocking requirements, manufacturing rate requirements, and so on for general North American distribution. In short, we want to be sure we are walking with a firm and steady tread before we begin to run.

It is particularly important that we work with good sales reps. To this end, we have contacted a number of people knowledgeable in the field (retailers, several small manufacturers of retail products, and two major wholesalers) for recommendations. We have received a number of responses and plan to hold interviews soon. We also plan an aggressive campaign of marketing at consumer electronics and related trade shows. To this end, we have designed and built an attractive display booth that will effectively demonstrate both products in operation. We plan to attend up to ten trade shows in the next six months and will use them as a showcase around which to meet potential sales reps, wholesalers, and customers. In addition, this will be our opportunity to introduce our products to the consumer electronics industry press. To this end, we have hired an experienced media consultant to work with us in developing a press package. She has already arranged for several articles about the Kinet-O-Scroll to appear in several popular electronics magazines.

DAY INTERNATIONAL, INC. anticipates expanding the principal sales areas toward the end of the first year of operation. As part of doing this, we hope our higher manufacturing volume will allow us to lower prices as well as to improve our products based on feedback from buyers. In subsequent years, DAY will continue to use sales reps and wholesalers as our main sales force, since they provide many advantages over employee salespeople. The principal advantage, of course, is that these people are

9

paid a commission (sales reps) or fixed percentage (wholesalers) of each sale but receive no salary.

Wholesalers have been included in the overall merchandising effort because they offer an established way to get our product onto the retailers' shelves. Many have been in business for years and offer retailers local delivery, computerized ordering, and other valuable services. They are expected to play a supportive role to our sales reps, who will have the primary responsibility to call on retailers, write orders, and so on. Many of these orders will be forwarded to the wholesaler to be filled (depending on the territory and our contractual relationship with the wholesaler), while others will be processed directly by DAY. It is important that the sales reps and the distributors work as a team. The representatives will be brought on early enough to have a strong voice in distributor selection.

G. Company Facilities

DAY INTERNATIONAL, INC. presently occupies a leased facility of slightly over 1,800 square feet at a very reasonable rental. We use this for both manufacturing and offices. We rent an additional 150 square feet of storage space nearby. There is no concern for the continuation of the lease on our principal location, as it contains three yearly options to renew at the same rate, plus a percentage increase equal to the yearly increase in the consumer price index. The existing space is adequate to support production of at least 400 Kinet-O-Scrolls per month. Nearby space is available for expansion at reasonable rates when we need it. An adequate work force of assembly workers and shipping room personnel is available. We expect to pay between $4.50 and $8.00 per hour to hourly employees, depending on their duties.

Several additions to the corporation's existing manufacturing equipment are required. Assuming, however, that the Kinet-O-Scroll production rate does not exceed 400 units per month, these expenditures will not exceed $30,000. When production increases above 400 units per month, we expect to show enough profit that a bank loan to finance more equipment will be easy to obtain. We can supply a potential investor with more details about these estimates upon request.

H. Product Development Status

Phillip Court began development work based on the Smith Patent in 2000. The idea was to develop operational prototypes of both the Kinet-O-Scroll and Kinet-O-Scope to prove manufacturing feasibility. After design and operation of several early prototypes of each product, a full set of engineering drawing and parts specifications was prepared for each in 2001. Parts were procured from suppliers and a number of units assembled. Next, units manufactured and assembled were subjected to life testing. With some minor modifications, an operational life of up to 4,488 hours without failure was achieved for the Kinet-O-Scope. This compares to an expected typical homeowner's usage of 1,000 to 2,000 hours. We are confident from these results that with some minor material changes, which are now in the works, and the introduction of improved mechanical alignment techniques, which we plan to do soon, a 10,000-hour design goal is achievable. This is our goal.

The Kinet-O-Scroll must, of course, be designed to meet far more stringent requirements. We aim to market a product that will last at least four years, even if used 24 hours a day. Tests based on time simulations indicate that we have achieved this goal.[2]

The Kinet-O-Scroll is already in production (units are available for testing), as described in Section I of this proposal, just below. The Kinet-O-Scope can be in production within 120 days after additional financing is obtained.

11

I. Production Status

The Kinet-O-Scroll is the first and only DAY product currently in production. Here is a summary of both how things are going on the shop floor and how our marketing efforts are developing, as of April 16, 2001.

Material: There is no difficulty obtaining parts for the Kinet-O-Scroll. The two parts with the longest order lead time are the motor and keyboard, which at present take about eight weeks to get. There has been some recent indication of possible stretch-outs on certain semiconductor products we have been getting on a next-day basis, but this is not expected to be a significant problem. Just in case, however, we have identified several alternative suppliers.

Inventories: The first 100 Kinet-O-Scroll units have been committed to production. At the time of this writing, 35 are complete and the remainder are 90% finished, requiring only cabinets and final assembly. All materials, with the exception of the cabinets, which should arrive in ten days, are in stock to complete these units, as well as an additional 100 units. The first 100 units are primarily for demonstration purposes. We will use several at trade shows, give others to the electronics press for evaluation, and use still others as samples for our sales reps and wholesalers.

Credit Terms: Although DAY has established 30-day terms with over half of its suppliers, we are presently on cash terms with the rest, due to our low cash position and because we are a new corporation with no proven credit history. We expect to arrange 30- to 60-day terms with all our suppliers within six months. New financing will help us accomplish this.

J. Product Selling Prices and Costs

The projections included in this business plan are based on several assumptions about product selling prices and costs.

Wholesale Selling Price

Kinet-O-Scroll	(Commercial Unit)	$550.00
Kinet-O-Scope	(Recreational Unit)	150.00

Direct (Variable) Cost of Each Unit

	Packaging	Direct Labor	Direct Material	Total Cost
Kinet-O-Scroll	$ 11.00	$ 24.00	$ 100.00	$ 135.00
Kinet-O-Scope	2.00	12.00	30.00	44.00

These figures do not allow for any corporation overhead, such as rent, management costs, and so on. They are based solely on the cost of producing each unit. All costs and selling prices have been developed through extensive market research and profitability analysis. They reflect the realities of the marketplace, as well as the price objectives of management.

K. Financial Statement and Projections

As DAY INTERNATIONAL, INC. is still in the start-up phase, we have yet to develop positive cash flow.[3] As the attached profit and loss projection and cash flow forecast indicate, however, we expect the corporation to begin to generate a positive cash flow and profit before the end of the first year of operations. To accomplish this, however, the corporation needs a total infusion of $150,000 equity capital. The founders have contributed half of that amount and are seeking additional investors for the balance. In exchange for a $75,000 investment, the investor would receive a one-third interest in the company. This would take the form of one-third of the stock in DAY INTERNATIONAL, INC. and one-third representation on the Board of Directors. As noted in Section B, above,

13

the existing shareholders are willing to design a shareholders' agreement to protect the interests and representation of the minority shareholders.

Profit projections show that if all goes according to plan, the investor can expect no return of his investment in the first year of operation and substantial profit in the second. (The accompanying profit and loss forecast shows a $338,255 profit for DAY INTERNATIONAL, INC. by the second year.) While the dividend policy of the corporation will be to pay modest dividends to investors in order to generate capital for growth, it can be expected that some of the available profits will be distributed to the shareholders. In addition, the investor can expect significant capital gains should the corporation make a public stock offering. The founders plan to do this after several years of profitable operations.

Warning to investors! Heretofore you have read an optimistic review of DAY INTERNATIONAL, INC. and its chances for future success. However, you should realize that the electronics business is a risky one. Many new products fail, while others succeed for a brief time, only to be supplanted by new technology, changing public taste, or foreign competition. While we believe we have planned carefully and well for each of these eventualities, we want to emphasize one thing loud and clear: Anyone who invests in DAY INTERNATIONAL, INC. is taking a substantial risk. While we believe chances of success are excellent, this is by no means guaranteed. In short, please do not invest money that you can't afford to lose.

Endnotes

1 Many small manufacturing operations will have a local marketing strategy, at least to start. Don't let the sort of marketing survey presented here intimidate you. The same sort of approach can be used for any manu-facturing business. For example, if you plan to make a better raisin-chocolate chip cookie or a crisper lemon tortilla chip for local distribution, think about ways you can convincingly tell a potential lender or investor that it will sell.

2 Test results are based on the brush/slip ring life-methods at three times normal speed, which have been independently monitored and are available upon request.

3 Since DAY is already in operation, it would be normal practice to include a balance sheet of operations to date. I do not do this here both because of space limitations and because we have not discussed balance sheets in the text. If your business is in operation, ask your bookkeeper or accountant to help you prepare a balance sheet and include it.

■

Chapter 8

Strategic Partners

One of the most practical and overlooked ways to finance an invention is to enlist strategic partners. A strategic partner is someone who typically plays a major and active role in designing, protecting, manufacturing, or marketing your invention—for example, an attorney, manufacturer, or prototype maker. In the case of an entrepreneurial inventor, a strategic partner commonly exchanges work for an interest in the inventor's company (as an equity investor). Less frequently, in the case of an inventor-for-royalties, a strategic partner will exchange work for a percentage of your anticipated royalties.

The term *strategic partner* is used to distinguish someone who contributes to the business from someone who merely invests money but does not participate in developing, protecting, or marketing your invention or in managing your company. I call the latter an investment partner.

Does a strategic partner dilute your ownership? Yes, like all equity investors, the strategic partner will own a piece of your invention business. But the strategic partner provides a potential benefit over other equity investors: participation, services, and advice. Your strategic partner is working hard to make sure that the investment succeeds. As with all equity investment, you have to ask the question, would you rather have half of something that succeeds rather than all of a dream that never materializes?

It's one of the long-standing traditions of capitalism that profits arise from the participation of many people providing different resources and skills.

Inventors—particularly entrepreneurial inventors—may benefit from a range of strategic partners. After all, the costs of prototyping, manufacturing, designing, and marketing a product can be enormous. Having strategic partners to assist in these tasks can save money and contribute to your success.

Below, I've set out some of the possible strategic partners you may enlist for your invention business.

Designers and Prototypers

I start with designers and prototypers before covering patent agents or attorneys for two reasons. First, the design and/or prototype are essential in determining whether you can acquire protection. If you have a design or a physical prototype, a patent agent or attorney will usually get a much better understanding of what you have invented and how it relates to prior art. Second, the design and/or prototype may help you refine your invention. It's often during the designing or prototyping process that a patentable feature is discovered. Sometimes this new feature is vital to the preparation of a strong patent. This is especially true in the case of "product" inventions, as distinguished from process or method inventions.

Designers

If you're undecided about bringing in a designer, keep in mind that the more defined and refined your invention is—that is, the more it looks like a finished product—the better are your chances for licensing or selling it. In addition, without a competent design, you will have a harder time getting a prototyper to create a model of your invention product—an essential for licensing and for soliciting investment. Finally, distinguishing the appearance of useful inventions has became crucial when competing manufacturers have products that do the same thing. For consumers, the ultimate buying decision often comes down to appearance.

The decision whether to seek a designer's assistance and/or cooperation as a strategic partner always depends on the product. Products aimed directly at the consumer are an obvious choice for making a designer a strategic partner.

> **EXAMPLE:** In 2001, Apple Computer released the "iPod," a small, stylish device that weighed 6.5 ounces and held approximately 1,000 songs. The iPod didn't do anything new—other devices allowed users to store and play back digital music. And it was expensive—$400 was considered unthinkable within the industry. But the iPod went on to dominate its category in sales numbers and revenue. The reason: design. It was the first device to combine three important elements for consumers: small size, large storage capacity, and a classy appearance. A novel feature that distinguished the iPod from its competitors was the "scroll wheel," a one-purpose switch with which the user could maneuver through song-lists, choose songs, or adjust volume. Unlike other "dials" or "wheels" on audio equipment, the iPod's wheel was "submerged" within the exterior, not protruding from it. All of these design elements transformed a product with an indistinguishable function from the rest of the pack.

An industrial designer will do most or all of the following:

- determine the shapes used in your invention
- decide dimensions and tolerances
- select or suggest materials
- select appropriate manufacturing methods
- supply a variety of peripheral items such as animated videos (virtual prototypes)
- prepare 3-D CAD drawings (drawings resulting in a digital file on disk or ready to email that can be used by the prototyper to automatically control machinery)
- assist in finding and selecting vendors (prototype and/or production), obtaining price quotations, and so forth, and
- in some cases, actually make the prototype.

Why not go directly to a prototyper and skip the designer? You may skip the designer if your invention is not sold to consumers, if design is not an issue in the sale or licensing of the invention, or if you already have a fixed vision of what it should look like.

Some industrial designers may also take on the task of producing (or supervising the production of) the prototype. The fees for design work can be fairly expensive ($5,000 to $10,000)—often costing much more than acquiring patent protection.

You can find industrial designers easily on the Internet. Sites such as the Industrial Designers Society of America (www.idsa.org) often post member credentials or job searches. You can find designers near you by using the yellow pages under the caption, "Designers, industrial." These listing are usually one-liners, that is, not display ads but listings of the bare essentials of name, address, and phone number. Some will have a few words about the kind of work they specialize in. Most of these design firms are very small, often one, two, or three people. You may also find industrial designers in the classified section of *Inventors' Digest* magazine (www.inventorsdigest.com).

Other than getting a beautiful product design on paper, you will have exacting dimensional input for making your prototype and may even save money on the prototype, because the digital design

data can be used to drive automatic machining, usually with significant savings over manual machining. The equipment for a process such as stereolithography, which creates a plastic model of the design from a CAD file, costs around a quarter of a million dollars and is found in job shops that specialize in this process. However, most prototypers who work with inventors use manual or semi-manual machines.

Many inventors rely on the prototyper to create the design and give the prototyper a crude sketch to start with, often without key dimensions or material specifications. The problem with approach is that, unfortunately, prototypers usually do not specialize in design and tend to favor function rather than cosmetics. It may work as described, but the appearance may not be appealing.

Prototypers

The job of a prototyper (sometimes referred to as a "model maker") is to produce a model of your invention so that other can see or interact with it. You may proceed with several prototypes; for example, you may build a very rough prototype that lets you know whether the invention works and then proceed to more sophisticated models—the ones built by professional prototypers—that look and operate like the final product.

As described above, a designer can be a worthwhile strategic partner for some inventors. For others, particularly in cases where the function—not the appearance—is the key and only real essential element in licensing or marketing, an inventor-friendly prototyper may be a better choice.

Moreover, the prototyper may prove more affordable, perhaps even bypassing the need for taking on a strategic partner and giving up equity. (Note, in some cases it may be the opposite—a designer may come up with inexpensive concept and sketches that are sufficiently detailed so that you can save money with the prototyper.)

It *is* possible for you to create your own prototype. To that end, I suggest looking at the *Encyclopedia of Model Making Techniques* by P. Quarto and Christopher Payne (Book Sales). Although it's a little hard to find, it's a comprehensive guide to constructing scale models with a thorough explanation of materials and techniques.

Finding prototype makers can be a challenge, depending on the field of invention, and will involve some web searching using search terms such as "prototype maker," "prototyper," and "model maker." You can also find inventor-friendly prototypers in the classified and display ads of *Inventors' Digest* (www.inventorsdigest.com) as well as in the yellow pages, usually listed under "model makers." Note, this listing is often loaded with suppliers of real estate models, so you have to phone each

listing and ask if they make invention prototypes. I have found the category "prototypes" in very few yellow page directories. JobShop.com (www.jobshop.com) lists many services for the inventor who is familiar with "rapid prototyping" processes, such as stereolithography,

Written Agreements for Designer and Prototypes

It is important to have a written agreement with the designer, as well as the prototyper, that any innovative features arising from the concept that you have provided become your property without further compensation to the designer and/or prototyper. Often a designer or prototyper will provide such an agreement.

Below is a sample agreement that you may find useful. This agreement offers the option of making the designer or prototyper a strategic partner. However, in order for it to work in that manner, you will need to create a separate agreement granting the partner an equity interest in your business. To do that, you should review the material below and then confer with an attorney. In the agreement below, you (the inventor) are referred to as the "Company." The designer or prototyper is the "Contractor."

Design/Prototype Agreement

This Agreement (the "Agreement") is made between _____ _____ ("Company"), and _____ ("Contractor").

Services. Contractor agrees to perform the following design and/or prototype services: _____ _____

The services shall be completed by the following date: _____

During the process, Contractor shall keep the Company informed of work in progress.

Payment. Company agrees to pay Contractor as follows:

Choose One

☐ $_____ for the services and acquisition of the rights provided below.

☐ For services valued at $_____ , Company grants to Contractor the consideration provided in the attached equity agreement, incorporated in this agreement by reference.

Assignment, Works Made for Hire. Contractor assigns to Company any trade secret, process, system, trademarks, or patentable creation (Innovations) created by or discovered or developed in whole or in part by Contractor as a result of any work performed by Contractor under this Agreement. Such Innovations shall be the sole and exclusive property of Company. Any works of authorship ("Works") commissioned pursuant to this Agreement shall be considered as works made for hire as that term is defined under U.S. copyright law. To the extent that any Works do not qualify as a work made for hire, Contractor hereby assigns and transfers to Company all rights in such Works.

Contractor agrees to sign and deliver to Company (either during or subsequent to commencing work) such documents as Company considers desirable to evidence: (1) the assignment to Company of all rights of Contractor, if any, in any such Innovation or Work, and (2) Company's ownership of such Innovations and Works.

Contractor Warranties. Contractor warrants that any Innovations or Works created by Contractor shall not infringe any intellectual property rights or violate any laws.

Confidential Information. For purposes of this Agreement, "Confidential Information" shall include all information or material that has or could have commercial value or other utility in the business in which Company is engaged. If Confidential Information is in written form, Company shall label or stamp the materials with the word "Confidential" or some similar warning. If Confidential Information is transmitted orally, Company shall promptly provide a writing indicating that such oral communication constituted Confidential Information.

Contractor's obligations not to disclose Confidential Information do not extend to information that is: (a) publicly known at the time of disclosure under this Agreement or subsequently becomes publicly known through no fault of Contractor; (b) discovered or created by Contractor prior to disclosure by Company; (c) otherwise learned by Contractor through legitimate means other than from Company or Company's representatives; or (d) is disclosed by Contractor with Company's prior written approval.

Contractor shall hold and maintain the Confidential Information of Company in strictest confidence for the sole and exclusive benefit of Company. Contractor shall carefully restrict access to Confidential Information to employees, contractors, and third parties as is reasonably required and only to persons subject to nondisclosure restrictions at least as protective as those set forth in this Agreement. Contractor shall return to Company any and all records, notes, and other written, printed, or tangible materials in its possession pertaining to Confidential Information immediately if Company requests it in writing.

Patent/Inventorship Rights. Contractor and Company recognize that under U.S. patent laws all patent applications must be filed in the name of the true inventor(s) of the invention. In the event that Contractor makes any patentable contributions relating to the design or creation of the prototype of the invention, Contractor agrees to be named as an application in any U.S. patent application regarding the invention that is the subject of this agreement, although actual ownership of such rights shall be controlled by the terms of this agreement.

Relationships. Nothing contained in this Agreement shall be deemed to constitute either party a partner, joint venturer, or employee of the other party for any purpose.

Severability. If a court finds any provision of this Agreement invalid or unenforceable, the remainder of this Agreement shall be interpreted so as best to effect the intent of the parties.

Integration. This Agreement expresses the complete understanding of the parties with respect to the subject matter and supersedes all prior proposals, agreements, representations, and understandings. This Agreement may not be amended except in a writing signed by both parties.

Waiver. The failure to exercise any right provided in this Agreement shall not be a waiver of prior or subsequent rights.

This Agreement and each party's obligations shall be binding on the representatives, assigns, and successors of such party. Each party has signed this Agreement through its authorized representative.

_____	_____
Contractor	Company
_____	_____
Signature	Signature
_____	_____
Typed or Printed Name	Typed or Printed Name
_____	_____
Date	Date

⚠ Patent law requires that any party who has contributed features that are claimed in the claims section of the patent must be listed as co-inventor on the patent application. To omit such a co-inventor is fraudulent and can lead to huge problems later, especially if your invention is very successful in the market and a competitor wants to invalidate your patent in court. The agreement requires that the contractor report any such innovations to you and indicates that all true inventors will be named on the application. Keep in mind that it is not common that a designer or prototyper contributes a patentable feature of an invention. However, these provisions are included in the event of such an occurrence.

Patent Agents and Attorneys

Inventors typically seek patent attorneys or patent agents—rather than designers, manufacturers, or marketing people—as strategic partners. This decision is usually because most uninitiated inventors begin their venture by filing for a patent (which, as discussed in Chapter 3, is often a mistake).

One reason inventors only pursue patent professionals as strategic partners is that the patenting phase of a venture is fairly well understood, whereas the designing, prototyping, manufacturing, and marketing phases are usually a mystery to the inventor. This is certainly the case

with the inventor-for-royalties, who often mistakenly overlooks certain strategic partners—believing that once the patent issues, all that is needed is to write a letter to companies and these companies will subsequently invite him to license it. (If only it were that simple.)

As noted in Chapter 3, a patent agent has passed the same test to be licensed by the United States Patent & Trademark Office as a patent attorney. However, although an agent may be equally qualified to draft your patent application, a patent agent cannot litigate or perform other services that an attorney is licensed to perform.

Enticing a patent agent or patent attorney to forgo his or her fee in exchange for a share in your company can be done, but it's challenging. So many inventors approach agents and attorneys with similar propositions that patent professionals—especially experienced professionals who have seen their share of failed inventions—may be hard to convince. As noted above, your invention, business proposal, and presentation will make the difference. (See Chapter 7 for more on business proposals.)

If you are an inventor-for-royalties who plans to license your invention, a patent agent or patent lawyer may be even more reluctant to participate with you as a strategic partner, since the sums involved in a license royalty are traditionally smaller than the potential windfall possible for the entrepreneurial inventor.

Unless you're prepared to offer a relatively large share of the royalties—for example, one-third, or even one-half—then this type of strategic partnering is unrealistic (If one-third sounds shocking, keep in mind that lawyers working on contingency—that is, they are only paid if the client's case succeeds—typically receive a third of the judgment.)

If you are an inventor-for-royalties who has also enlisted the designer and prototyper as strategic partners, you will end up with very little for yourself. Consider that the typical royalty is around 5%. Your attorney would insist on 2% (40% of the 5%). Would you and your two other partners (the designer and prototyper), be satisfied each getting one percent of the manufacturer's invoice (wholesale) price? Unless you have invented the next Xerox machine, there may not be enough in each slice of the pie to attract and adequately compensate each partner. The point here is that, for the inventor-for-royalties, sharing royalties with partners is generally not sufficiently profitable for them or you to be practical. If you are an entrepreneurial inventor, however, even relatively small percentages of ownership may offer attractive opportunities if the invention has multimillion dollar sales potential.

Licensing Agents

This section only deals with inventors who license inventions (the inventor-for-royalties). These inventors need help in three ways—designing, protecting, and licensing—and it is the latter task in which they are most likely to acquire a strategic partner, usually in the form of a licensing agents (sometimes called an "invention broker"). (Note: For information about locating a potential manufacturer/licensee see "The Proprietary Products Manufacturer," below)

Licensing agents receive a percentage of all sales (royalties) in return for soliciting and closing a licensing deal. The agent's payment will probably be somewhere between twenty and fifty percent of the total royalty paid by the manufacturer, including, of course, a percentage of any upfront bonus or advance on royalties. By acquiring an ongoing interest in their services (versus receiving a one-time payment for their services), licensing agents are, by nature, strategic partners. I have never heard of an agent who wants less than fifteen percent of the royalties. Generally they want a lot more. There is no standard percentage. And many inventions will never get licensed at any price.

That said, I want to emphasize that although, from the inventor's point of view, a licensing agent may look and act like a "partner," the inventor should not form a partnership, venture, or other business ownership relationship with an agent. Limit your arrangement to licensing. (A sample licensing agreement is provided below). If your relationship with the agent is viewed as a partnership, the agent may bind you in ways other than licensing or, in some cases, claim rights to profit from any inventions derived from your ideas or even from inventions that you may later bring to your company.

The length of your licensing arrangement (and your obligation to pay the agent) will likely be tied to the length of your patent. A utility patent runs out twenty years from the date of filing, after which your invention is then officially in the public domain, and anyone can legally make it and sell it (although you may retain rights to derivative inventions).

Some agents may charge an upfront fee as well as receive a part of the royalties. This fee is said to cover initial research, and, arguably, in many cases it may be justified—for example if the agent, after spending a few days and several phone calls, maybe even a few road trips, discovers that something very similar to your invention was tried a few years ago and flopped. None of the appropriate potential licensees will be even remotely interested.

An argument against justifying an upfront fee is the fact that some agents may become self-corrupted by the relatively easy money they receive in upfront fees. The fee may also make you question whether the agent is ethical. If in doubt about whether an agent or invention broker is ethical, review "Watch Out for Scam Marketing Companies" in Chapter 3.

Should you pay upfront money to a marketing agent who refuses to work solely on commission? If you are satisfied with the agent's references and the amount is under two thousand dollars, it may worthwhile. But if the upfront costs are higher and you learned about the agent from a TV ad, you'd be better off taking your money to Las Vegas to gamble; the returns are much, much better.

When in doubt about using an invention broker, ask, "Out of a hundred inventions submitted for your consideration, how many do you accept and attempt to license?" An ethical agent will likely reject, out of hand, at least four out of five due to either the anticipated difficulty of licensing or the nature of the invention being foreign to the agent. The agent who takes on a higher percentage of inventions is more likely to be ineffective (due to the poor marketability prospects of many, if not most, inventions) or, worse, a scam artist.

You can find legitimate licensing agents in *Inventors' Digest*. But remember my warnings, review Chapter 3 for more information about scam marketing agents, and ask the questions I have suggested. As the late Tomas Herschfeld once said, "When using experts, ask until they stutter."

Licensing Agent Agreement

Below is a sample agreement you can use with a licensing agent (or compare to the agreement presented by your proposed agent). Although the letter format used in this agreement is less formal, it is just as enforceable as a non-letter contract. If you don't want to use the letter format, simply remove the date and salutation. Note, it is necessary to attach a detailed description of the invention as an attachment. It may only be a few paragraphs, but this description will provide the basis for the agent to license your invention.

Manufacturers

Manufacturers can be divided into two basic categories: job shops and proprietary products manufacturers. A job shop manufactures to its customer's specifications; it has no products of its own. As such, it makes an ideal strategic partner. A proprietary products manufacturer produces products for which it obtains the rights, controls the design, and controls the marketing. It may be a candidate for strategic partnering, but you need sufficient clout to enter into such an arrangement. A proprietary products manufacturer is more likely to license your invention (or to buy it outright). For that reason, the proprietary products manufacturer is usually pursued by the inventor-for-royalties, not the entrepreneurial inventor.

The Job Shop

If all you need is tooling and manufacturing—and no marketing assistance—than a job shop will make a good strategic partner. Here are couple of examples. Several years ago I was involved in a startup company based on my patent for a bicycle transmission (US Pat. 4,820,244). One of my vendors was a job shop that was managed by an astute fellow who had invented a filler spout for gasoline tanks on garden machines such as lawn mowers, weed whackers, and so forth. He spent about $100,000 developing,

Licensing Agent Agreement

Date: _____

Dear: _____

This letter sets forth the terms and conditions of the agreement (the "Agreement") between _____
("Inventor") and _____
("Agent"). Inventor is the owner of licensing rights to various processes and technologies, referred to in this Agreement as the "Properties" and described more fully in Attachment A to this Agreement. Inventor agrees to have Agent serve as an exclusive representative and Agent for the Properties within the toy hobby, and game market which includes but is not limited to toys, games, hobbies, and crafts products.

Obligations of Agent. Agent shall perform the following services:

Evaluation and Consultation. Agent will identify potential licensees for the Properties within the toy, hobby, and game market.

Sales Representation. Agent shall serve as Inventor's exclusive Agent for the exploitation of the Properties within the toy, hobby and game industry. As Inventor's Agent, Agent shall contact and solicit potential licensees or purchasers and present and communicate potential license information between the parties.

Negotiation of Agreements. Agent shall work in association with Inventor in the negotiation of sales, licensing, option, or other agreements transferring licensing rights to the Properties.

Obligations of Inventor. Inventor will consult with licensees of the Properties and provide technical assistance and support for the Properties.

Payments. Inventor agrees that all income paid as a result of any agreement solicited or negotiated by Agent for the Properties (the "Properties Income") shall be paid directly to Agent and that Agent shall issue payments to Inventor within ten (10) days of Agent's receipt of any Properties Income along with any client accountings as provided by the licensee. As compensation for the services provided above, Agent shall receive _____ (_____%) of any Properties Income including, but not limited to, any advances, guarantees, or license fees. The provisions of this Section shall survive any termination of this Agreement.

Proprietary Rights; Indemnity. Inventor represents and warrants that it has the power and authority to enter into this Agreement and that it is the owner of all proprietary rights, whether they are patent, copyright, or otherwise and that the Properties are not in any way based upon any confidential or proprietary information derived from any source other than Inventor. Because Agent is relying on these representations, Inventor agrees to indemnify Agent and its assignees and hold them harmless from any losses or damages resulting from third-party claims arising from a breach of these representations or from Agent's solicitation or representations regarding the Properties. Inventor's indemnification of Agent shall survive any termination of this Agreement.

Disclaimer. Nothing in this Agreement shall be interpreted by Inventor as a promise or guarantee as to the outcome of any solicitation or negotiation by Agent on behalf of Inventor or the Properties. Any representations as to the likelihood of success regarding exploitation of the Properties are expressions of opinion only. Agent is free to conduct business other than on Inventor's behalf, including business or agency relationships with third parties in the same field as Inventor.

Confidentiality. The parties acknowledge that each may be furnished or may otherwise receive or have access to information that relates to each other's business and the affairs of the respective clients (the "Information"). The parties agree to preserve and protect the confidentiality of the Information and all physical forms. Information relating to the terms, provisions, and substance of this Agreement shall remain within the strictest confidence of both parties, and neither party shall disclose such information to third parties without the prior written consent of the other.

Termination. This Agreement may be terminated at any time at the discretion of either Inventor or Agent, provided that written notice of such termination is furnished to the other party thirty (30) days prior to such termination. If this Agreement is terminated by Inventor, and, within twelve (12) months of termination, Inventor enters into an agreement to option, license, sell, or otherwise exploit the Properties with any company solicited or contacted by Agent on Inventor's behalf, Inventor agrees to pay the fees established in this Agreement.

Attachments and Exhibits. Any material contained in an attachment, exhibit, or addendum to this Agreement shall be incorporated in this Agreement. From time to time, the parties may revise the information specified in the attachments or exhibits. Such revisions, if executed by both parties, shall be incorporated in this Agreement and shall be binding on the parties.

General. Nothing contained in this Agreement shall be deemed to constitute either Agent or Inventor as a partner, joint venturer, or employee of the other party for any purpose. This Agreement may not be amended except in writing signed by both parties. Each and all of the rights and remedies provided for in this Agreement shall be cumulative. No waiver by Agent of any right shall be construed as a waiver of any other right. If a court finds any provision of this Agreement invalid or unenforceable as applied to any circumstance, the remainder of this Agreement shall be interpreted so as best to effect the intent of the parties. This Agreement shall be governed by and interpreted in accordance with the laws of the State of _____ . Any controversy or claim arising out of or relating to this Agreement, or the breach of this Agreement, shall be settled by arbitration in accordance with the rules of American Arbitration Association, and judgment upon the award rendered by the arbitrator(s) may be entered in any court having jurisdiction. The prevailing party shall have the right to collect from the other party its reasonable costs and attorneys' fees incurred in enforcing this agreement. Any such arbitration hearing shall include a written transcript of the proceedings and a written explanation for any final determination. This Agreement expresses the complete understanding of the parties with respect to the subject matter and supersedes all prior proposals, agreements, representations, and understandings.

If these terms and conditions are agreeable, please sign and execute both copies of this Agreement and return one copy to Agent.

Inventor: **Agent:**

_____   _____
Date   Date

_____   _____
Signature   Signature

_____   _____
Typed or Printed Name   Typed or Printed Name

_____   _____
Title   Title

packaging, and attempting to market his invention, which was excellent. It solved the problem of automatically shutting off the flow of gasoline simply by lifting the container away from the filler hole. Unfortunately, it was unsuccessful, because the inventor was unable to market the product, and, as far as I know, he still has hundreds of these filler spouts sitting in storage.

I also speak from direct experience. When banks first decided to have their customers wait in a common queue and then beckon them to the next available teller, the tellers were left to their own devices for alerting their next customer. A friend and I developed a flashing light that shone on the ceiling. It flashed five times and shut off. All who saw it agreed that it was a beautiful and functional device. Did I get it to the market? No. I hadn't a clue as to how to sell it. My job shop at that time (Short-run Precision Fabricators in Laverne, California) did a great job of manufacturing but lacked an understanding as to the marketing of proprietary products.

Job shops seldom have proprietary products of their own. But, having been a job shop founder/operator, and knowing others in this kind of business, I know that many of us wanted proprietary products and would have been open to a deal had an inventor come along with a hot product that we had the skills and equipment to make.

The Proprietary Products Manufacturer

A proprietary products manufacturer is already manufacturing products—possibly similar to yours—and usually has a marketing organization in place. For example, General Motors, Kitchen-Aid, and Dell Computers are all proprietary products manufacturers. These are distinguished by their control of the design of the product and their ownership (or licensing) of any intellectual properties that may apply.

Thus, the inventor-for-royalties is not pursuing a manufacturer as a strategic partner (who acquires equity) but as a potential licensee. You will obviously be seeking a manufacturer that sells products that are similar, complementary, or an accessory to your invention. (You certainly won't approach a company that has products foreign to your invention, right?) Manufacturing may either take place on the premises or be subcontracted.

The challenge with a proprietary products company (or any potential licensee) is convincing the company to take your product on. Many such companies suffer from NIH syndrome (not invented here) and are unlikely to consider your invention since it was not conceived within. Jealousy may prevail, and an unfair evaluation of your invention by the second-tier managers may cause it to be voted out.

Some proprietary manufacturers such as 3M are receptive to invention submissions, but, of course, on their terms. The inventor typically signs away all rights except those conferred by his patent.

Finding Manufacturers and Licensees

You can find both job shops and proprietary manufactures by using the Thomas Register, available online (www .thomasregister.com) or in print format, *Thomas Register of American Manufacturers* (Thomas Register Publishing). The Thomas Register lists manufacturers by subject and provides profiles and phone numbers.

Job shops get business mainly by advertising their service and waiting for customers to approach them. You can find them at Jobshop.com (www.jobshop .com). Once you register, you can find a lot of information on processes, and a long list of job shops for the various specialties.

Proprietary manufacturers are already visible in the marketplace, and you can find them using traditional methods—for example, scouting retail locations that sell products similar to yours and identifying manufacturers; reviewing trade magazines, trade journals, or industry newsletters; or performing Internet research.

SIC Codes

Most manufacturers utilize a system known as the Standard Industrial Classification Code (SIC). The SIC is a four-digit number created by the Department of Commerce and is used to classify a business by the type of work it does. For example, if you invented a product to be worn while handling explosives, you might review companies classified as 1795, which is the code for the Wrecking and Demolition Industry. If you invented a timer for video cameras, you would check companies classified as 3651 for Video Equipment and Household Audio. The SIC is helpful when searching since most corporate directories, whether in print, digital, or online form, include an index of SIC codes. You can obtain SIC code information at the North American Industry Classification System website (www .naics.com).

One of the best ways to locate these manufacturers is via trade publications. Almost every trade or business has a journal or directory published for the benefit of the companies competing within the trade. Directories are particularly helpful because they contain indexes that may allow fast cross-referencing of product or service titles. For example, members of the toy and hobby industry subscribe to the trade publication *Playthings*. This publication also distributes an annual "Buyer's Directory" issue. By reviewing the Buyer's Directory, it may be possible to quickly locate manufacturers. You can locate manufacturer/ licensee information in *Gale Directory of Publications, Information Industry Directory, National Directory of Catalogs, Oxbridge Directory of Newsletters,* or *The Standard Periodical Directory.*

Dividing the Pie With Strategic Partners

Probably the most important question that arises when granting equity to strategic partners is what percentage of the shares of the company the inventor should grant to each partner.

There is one simple answer to this question: As little as possible while still respecting the profit motive of the investor. Here is my reasoning: If you give up a big chunk of stock to early partners, you almost certainly won't be able to attract the right capital later on. Thus, when your product is ready to "roll out," you will be severely handicapped by not having sufficient finance, and your enterprise will remain "small potatoes," that is, an interesting little business that could have made it big. This is especially true if your product has enough profit potential to attract competitors that may take advantage of a small, undercapitalized company.

Carried to its extreme, you might believe that an offer of one percent of your company is fair. Not so. An offer of one percent would likely insult the intelligence of any potential strategic partner and kill any deal before it got beyond the exploratory conversation. True, one percent of General Motors would make anyone rich beyond imagination, of course. But your invention isn't a Chevrolet, and none of your potential partners is going to wait several decades until compounding growth makes them enormously rich.

Ten percent of a startup company is the kind of minimum talking figure that might attract me if I were a designer or patent attorney. But only if that ten percent were in some equitable relationship to the amount of stock you claimed for your own, as the founder, and for the other partners. Ideas are like flies at a garbage dump. A raw idea is essentially worthless until it matures into an invention that has physical form, such as a prototype, or at least a credible design on paper or computer screen, and is judged as patentable by a patent professional. Perhaps the "idea person" is entitled to significantly more than the other main partners because he or she has not only dreamed up the idea but also is orchestrating the venture and will act as the prime mover to its conclusion. But if I were the only partner (let's say, again, the designer) with ten percent, and you wanted to hog ninety percent, I'd probably tell you to get lost.

A rationale that makes some sense, at least to me, is this: The entrepreneur is both inventor and orchestrator and is entitled to at least twice the shares that any other individual partner receives, but no more than five times. (This assumes that your are engaging highly competent partners who will be an ongoing asset to your corporation.) You must ask yourself what are the limits of resentment from the other partners, as well as what appears most enriching to you.

The reason for limiting the issuance of shares is because the need for much larger amounts of money lies ahead if your invention has extraordinary potential. At some point ahead you will need cash from an angel investor, or possibly even a venture capital firm.

Angels (the independent investors I will discuss in Chapter 9) are somewhat unpredictable when it comes to the percentage of stock that they will demand in exchange for finance. Some angels will want 51 percent so that they can control the company and kick out any partners who are not effective (or even kick out some who are effective in order to kick in their own people). Other angels will want a substantial chunk, but not control, preferring that the control, and the burden of succeeding, remain with the entrepreneur and his or her strategic partners. Thus, it seems prudent

to never yield more than a total of 49 percent except in the most desperate circumstances. In other words, you and all of your partners should hold at least 51 percent forever, if possible. (The more successful you become, the less likely you'll be able to hold onto that 51 percent. Not necessarily a bad situation.)

The mechanism for "dividing the pie" is that of issuing stock or shares. For example, suppose you start out with a declaration that your corporation has 100 shares. These shares represent its total value at the time you incorporate. The true value may be nothing or even negative at this time, but that's not the point. Now, you take in three equal partners who are each given 10 shares in exchange for their contributions. You hold 21 shares. The remaining 49 shares are held "in the treasury," which may be only an envelope in your milk-crate file at this time. This is an example of the humble beginning of a corporation that at least has defined who owns how much.

I'm not saying here that this is the best way to set it up. You need expert advice from an attorney and perhaps an accountant when the time comes to divide your equity. But the principle I have illustrated is sound. If you want me as a partner, and I have a declaration signed by you that says you own twice as much as I do (plus 1 percent), I am going to sense the fairness of this arrangement and may be satisfied. Such declaration may be a "pre-stock memorandum"—a letter addressed to me that states that when stock is formally issued, my shares will be half as much (adjusted for the 1 percent) as yours, and so on. Again, get legal advice before issuing any pre-stock memoranda.

Okay, that's a reasonable starting point. Now, how much should you, personally, hold if you have done quite a bit of research and development work? Let's say that you are so woefully lacking in "seed money" (the money it takes to get the venture to the point where you are ready to attract an angel investor) that you decide to attract the following strategic partners: designer, prototyper, patent professional, manufacturer, and marketer. That's stretching things pretty thin, of course. But it could be done.

The first question that must be answered is which of the persons or companies performing these vital functions should be welcomed as strategic partners, and which should be hired for pay. The easy answer is to pay them all and take in no partners, but this violates our scenario of the inventor who does not have sufficient seed money to get through the requisite steps prior to attracting serious capital from an angel. At this preliminary stage we must balance the cost of delays caused by accumulating money against the desire to retain as much of our company as possible. The complexity of the invention is a major factor. Usually there is a close

correspondence between the complexity of the invention and cost of each of the disciplines required to launch it, especially the disciplines of design engineering and tooling.

If the invention requires a lot of design work, drawings, and perhaps two or three successive prototypes before it evolves to a "looks like, works like" (the eventual product) model, you will have to consider including at least the designer, and maybe the prototyper, as strategic partners. The patent agent or attorney may have an ongoing role as the legal protector of the present invention, whatever it evolves into, and peripheral products. And because of the relatively large cost of the patent compared to the design work in the typical case, the patent agent or attorney will probably feel entitled to more shares than the designer. Here is where it gets sticky. How do you assess the value of each contribution and award stock commensurately? Probably the fairest way is to solicit price quotes from each potential contributor before proposing the idea of exchanging stock for work. Then, divide the pie according to the monetary equivalent portion of each contributor.

How about you? Do the same thing for yourself. Assign a value to your time based on the skill level demanded, and add in something for having the idea or thinking up the invention so that you come out with a slice of the pie that will sound reasonable and fair to the other partners. The factor by which you multiply the typical or average of the partners in order to assign your own share depends also on the level to which you have taken the development of your invention and the number of partners. For example: If you have only one partner, let's say a marketer, and you want 41 percent as against the marketer's 10 percent (for a total of 51), the 41 is a much larger portion of the total than if you have three other partners, each at 10 percent, and you are only taking 21 percent. In the latter case you, the inventor, are only taking one-fifth (plus a bit) of the whole. You appear less greedy as a one-fifth owner of your own invention.

Still another consideration is the extent to which a partner's function is traditionally a percentage of the selling price. Marketing, for example, generally takes at least half of the selling price of most retail items that are priced at less than a couple of hundred dollars. By the time the retailer (at about 40 percent or more), plus the distributor, plus the sales rep, plus advertising allowance, are all added up, the total portion of the retail selling price can easily add up to 60 or even 65 percent. Thus, marketing people may come to think of their function as the hub of the corporate wheel.

Early in my career I was a corporate systems analyst responsible for inventory and production control systems. The Marketing Director tried to talk me into transferring into Marketing to do research for him. This was many years ago, but I still remember Ken Waldron's words (maybe not exactly, but close enough): "Marketing is the essence of our business. As long as we have blueprints we can farm out manufacturing anywhere, but we have to control marketing; our success depends on it." My point is that you may encounter this kind of argument from any of the potential partners, and you must think through the importance of each to your business and be ready with an answer. (And maybe Ken Waldron was right. Maybe without competent marketing your invention or mine is just another "great idea" that will sit on the back burner until it is as obsolete as an eight-track tape player.)

In any event, fairness is an essential element for success. Whether glory or gold motivates the partners, each must feel total dedication to the venture for it to succeed, and that dedication will likely erode if an essential partner feels he or she is not apportioned fairly.

■

Chapter 9

Angel Investment

As I coach inventors and listen to their problems and frustrations, I hear the same theme again and again: "I don't have any money. Certainly there must be people who are willing to finance my great idea, aren't there?"

The answer is yes. In fact, there is more money available for truly great ideas today than ever before. One reason for this is that corporations are regularly downsizing, and many men and women find themselves either looking for a job or looking for a business to go into. In such times not only is the job market highly competitive, but the younger men and women—especially those who have recently graduated from college—are willing to work for less money than their seasoned counterparts. This significantly increases the pool of older workers who can't find a job and are considering starting their own business.

Many of these downsized and seasoned workers have been compensated by way of early retirement, also known as a buyout. Many have cash or stock that can be converted to cash. And many have always wanted to get into their own business. (One author says that instead of an up-to-date resume in their top desk drawer, executives nowadays have a business plan.)

Senior executives are contemplating their next move. Those in their fifties often have paid off their mortgage, put their kids through school, and acquired most of the high-tech "toys" that give them comfort. What they need now is a fulfilling sense of purpose—something more than television or fishing or gardening—to challenge their time and years of experience.

These men and women often take financial risks in startup enterprises, and when they do so, they join a community of investors referred to as angels, a term borrowed from the high-rollers who finance Broadway shows. These angel investors (estimated to number 300,000 to 400,000) account for the approximately $30 to $50 billion invested directly into financing startup businesses.

In this chapter I discuss angel investors in general and for purposes of solicitation. I separate angels into two groups: those within your geographic area (I call them "nearby angels"), and those outside your area ("remote angels").

The Angel Spectrum

The average angel investor is 47 years old with an annual income of $90,000, has a net worth of $750,000, and invests $37,000 per venture. (See Kate Lister and Tim Harnish, *Finding Money* (Wiley).) But this "average angel" is not really representative of the angel community, because angel investors fall into several categories. Knowing the various types of angels, their personalities, and their investing strategies may help you when soliciting investment.

Various studies have been done on the angel personality, and they're summarized by Mark Osnabrugee and Robert J. Robinson in their book *Angel Investing: Matching Start-Up Funds With Start-up Companies* (Jossey-Bass). Some analysts categorize angels in relation to their source of income—for example, professional angels (doctors, lawyers, accountants, and so on) or corporate angels (ex-corporate executives who use early retirement funds to invest). Others use amusing nicknames—for example, Cousin Randy (someone who only invests in their own family businesses), Dr. Kildare (professional investors), and Daddy Warbucks (the wealthiest angels). One of the best breakdowns of angel personalities is in *Angel Financing: How to Find and Invest in Private Equity* (Wiley), in which authors Gerald Benjamin and Joel Margulis outline nine types of angel investors. They include:

- **The Value-Added Investor.** This is an experienced hands-on investor who invests close to home in order to guarantee direct involvement in the business. This investor looks for passionate, persistent management.
- **The Deep-Pocket Investor.** This investor—often someone who's built a company from scratch—invests in industries or products with which he's familiar, wants a high rate of average annual return on investment (ROI) of usually 50% or more, and often requires a seat on the board.
- **The Consortium of Individual Investors.** Sometimes a loose group of private investors with startup experience invests as a group. When they do, they prefer technology or product companies and often align themselves with deep-pocket investors.
- **The Partner Investor.** In their book, Benjamin and Margulis categorize the Partner Investor as a "buyer in disguise"—someone with a strong desire for control who usually wants to be president of the company
- **The Family of Investors.** These are related individuals—often Asian—who pool their money and invest it in nearby startups with the guidance of a skilled family member.
- **The Barter Investor.** This investor is a cousin to the strategic partner. (See Chapter 8). Instead of providing cash for equity, the Barter Investor provides items your company needs to buy.
- **The Socially Responsible Private Investor**. This investor—often the recipient of inherited wealth—seeks a reasonable ROI but is equally interested in companies with altruistic personal values.
- **The Unaccredited Private Investor.** The least experienced of the angels, this investor chooses ventures close to home, likes to get to know management personally, and wants a return within five years (maybe less).
- **The Manager Investor**. According to Benjamin and Margulis, this affluent

angel is really seeking to "buy their next job." The Manager Investor concentrates on one investment and is less tolerant of risk than other angels.

What Motivates an Angel to Invest?

One thing that distinguishes an angel from a financial institution or a venture capital fund is that the angel is not in the business of giving money to businesses. That is, these wealthy people don't have to invest. They can just as easily not place their money into a risky investment. Therefore, in order to successfully solicit money, it helps to understand what motivates an angel to part with money and place it into a high-risk venture. Below are five factors that influence an angel's decision to invest:

- **Desire for $$$$$$.** Angels understand that one out of three of their investments will fail. But, as for the others—the successes—they expect to cash out within seven years (often less), and they expect at the minimum a 25% annual return on their investments. Note, your agreement with an angel will often specify the terms of a payout.
- **Dreaming of huge markets.** An angel who invests in a new product gambles on the fact that the market for it will be bigger than big; it will be huge—so huge that a larger

company will step in and purchase the enterprise.
- **Looking for a fun ride.** One of the main reasons angels participate in high-risk equity investments is the thrill of the game. Interesting products, stimulating people, and the possibility of adventure stir many angel hearts.
- **Interested in a great team.** Angels want to see experienced, passionate management. Angel investors, when surveyed, ranked team quality as a decisive factor in whether to invest—consistently ranking it higher in importance than the company's business plan.
- **A great proposal.** Angels want to see encouraging, honest, reliable paperwork. Though not the most important factor (see above), your proposal and accompanying presentation are the door opener for angel investment.

Due Diligence

It's not enough that an angel investor likes you, your product, your proposal, and your team. Just as you wouldn't buy a house without an inspection, angel investors will not invest without performing some form of "due diligence"—a process by which the angel investigates the facts, risks, and potential value of your business. (Note: A more sophisticated form of due diligence is performed when venture capitalists invest and when a company prepares for an initial public offering (IPO).) An angel's due diligence usually includes:

- **Verifying facts in your business proposal or plan.** Angels will not rely on your word regarding financials or marketing; they will want to see all supporting information and may conduct their own investigations and prepare their own financials.

- **Interviewing your friends and associates.** Angels often want to speak with everyone associated with the business as well as your acquaintances and people with whom you have worked in the past.

- **Examining your team.** Your management team ranks as one of the top concerns for an investor. Your investor will want some assurance that people who manage your invention business know what they're doing and hopefully have a successful track record with similar ventures.

- **Digging up background information about you.** A lot of personal information—including criminal records, civil judgments, bad debts—is available to anyone willing to pay for an Internet background check. There's little sense trying to hide any of that from potential investors.

- **Examining your product and patent.** Also as part of the due diligence, an investor will likely investigate your product, your patent, and the industry in which you are engaged. Expect an investor to have a patent attorney to determine the enforceability and scope of your patent— that is, how broad your claims are and whether it will be difficult stopping others from imitating your innovation.

- **Studying the competition**. An angel investor will study your actual and prospective competitors and will also examine the channel in which you compete—for example, to determine if there will be problems with distribution.

- **Learning about current owners.** A new investor will want to know about existing investors and their ownership interests. For example, how much will a new investor diminish an existing investor's ownership?

How Much Equity Does an Angel Want?

Angels want a piece of your business— usually represented by corporate shares. According to Osnabrugee and Robinson (*Angel Investing: Matching Start-Up Funds With Start-up Companies* (Jossey-Bass)), on average, angel investors typically receive 21% equity in the businesses in which they invest. However, of course, an angel who wants to control the business will seek a majority stake.

The actual amount an angel wants from your company depends on how much the investor is placing into the business and how your invention business is valued. Typically, the investment equals a percentage of the business value. So, if your invention business is valued at $100,000, an angel would, as a very general rule, expect to pay $25,000 for a 25% ownership interest.

Obviously, there are a few challenges here. One is to determine the appropriate market value for your invention business—a difficult task considering the speculative nature of many inventions, especially inventions that have not yet been market-tested. Another challenge is not only to determine what the company is worth at the time of investment, but also to consider its value at the time when the angel plans to cash in—for example, the value of the company when it is sold in five years.

An investor may use various methods to value your company. These include

- income-based valuation—placing a value on projected income,
- asset-based valuation—valuing your business based on its assets minus liabilities, or
- market-multiplier valuation—multiplying your income (or projected income) by a certain factor common to businesses within your industry.

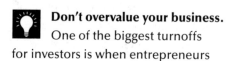 **Don't overvalue your business.** One of the biggest turnoffs for investors is when entrepreneurs overvalue their venture. Wishful thinking is fine, but don't let it drift into your spreadsheets and other financial information.

 One angel may be better than many angels. Always keep in mind that angels often want to control, or at least have an influence over, how their investment is handled. That means they usually want a hand in the business management. A group of angels that are united in their mission may be beneficial, but, as a general rule, having many investors can often lead to confusion and bickering. If possible, limit angel investment to a minimum of one or two people.

There is no shortage of business appraisers available to examine and value your business. It's also possible that you and your investors can agree upon a valuation based on your own analysis, without the need for an appraisal. That should provide a baseline, at least for the first round of your investors.

But keep in mind that the investor is going to be looking for a return between 20% and 50% annually. So, if an investor puts in $250,000 for a one-quarter interest of a business valued at $1,000,000 and expects to cash out in five years with a 40% per year return, your business would have to be worth $5,400,000 in five years in order for the angel to receive $1,350,000 (a 40% return on $250,000 over 5 years).

As you can see, when making these calculations, you and your investors are actually making two valuations. One is the amount at the time you are selling equity; the other is based on a rate of return over time. If this seems confusing, it may be time to seek the advice of an attorney and an accountant.

Also, angels may want more than an ownership interest. They may want management power, a right for future financing—for example, to buy more shares at a fixed price or to prevent their ownership rights from being diluted—and/or some degree of control over the venture. Making these decisions may be beyond the skill of an inventor. Seek advice when you are asked to make concessions such as creating voting classes, ceding control or power to board members, or granting management control, particularly if you intend to keep a majority interest and control over the board.

Don't Violate Securities Laws

If you're a corporation, limited liability company, or limited partnership, you'll need to comply with federal (as well as state) securities laws when you offer ownership interests to people who will not be actively working in the business.

Securities laws are meant to protect investors from unscrupulous business owners. They require businesses to regis-

ter the sale of certain kinds of ownership interests with the federal Securities and Exchange Commission (SEC)—a time-consuming process that involves extra legal and accounting fees.

Fortunately, you can skip the registration process, because of securities "exemptions." For example, SEC rules don't require a corporation to register a "private offering," which is a nonadvertised sale of stock to either:

- a limited number of people (generally 35 or fewer), or
- those who, because of their net worth or income earning capacity, can reasonably be expected to take care of themselves in the investment process ("accredited investors").

So, if you meet these criteria—fewer than 35 investors and/or accredited investors—you will qualify for the primary exemption. In order to guarantee that you will avoid problems regarding securities laws, here are three "Don'ts" and one "Do":

- **Don't** conceal, lie, or exaggerate about the investment opportunity. Always provide potential investors with everything that is available for them to make a knowledgeable decision. When in doubt, disclose, disclose, disclose.
- **Don't** make public advertisements of your investment opportunity.
- **Don't** accept investments (or any payment for interest in your invention) unless the transaction is exempt from security registration

requirements. If in doubt, speak with an attorney.

- **Do** include the following notice on all solicitations, business proposals, and business plans: "Investing in this enterprise involves considerable risk and should not be done unless you are prepared to lose the complete investment. Estimates of projected income or revenue are speculative, and this company does not presently have the capital required to meet such projections."

You can learn more information about SEC exemptions at the SEC website (www.sec.gov). A quick way to research your state's exemption rules is to go to the home page of your state's securities agency, which typically posts the state's exemptions rules and procedures. To find your state securities agency, go to your Secretary of State's website.

Nearby Angels

According to an SBA report, seven out of ten small business investments are made within 50 miles of the investor's home or office. In other words, the vast majority of angels are contributing to ventures that they can drive to and physically observe.

Nearby angels include family, friends, retired coworkers, and other persons in your geographic area who have money to invest but who may not be professional investors. These angels could be your dentist, doctor, lawyer, or accountant and may not think of themselves as angels in the usual financial sense. But they fit within the description of the angel investor—often bored with their current source of income, receptive to a new financial adventure, particularly with someone they know, and comfortable investing $35,000 or more in the right business. They may be willing to invest in a risky venture if it offers the prospect of a high rate of return on their investment, particularly if it provides an opportunity to engage in a creative or inspiring venture.

EXAMPLE: Several years ago I owned a small manufacturing business in the Los Angeles suburb of Laverne. I produced precision sheet metal products such as cabinets for electronic controls, chassis, brackets, and so forth. One of my products was a pair of mounting brackets for a spinnaker pole that was used on luxury sailboats. These were very classy brackets made from heavy aluminum finished with gold anodizing. The fellow who had designed the brackets owned a sailboat, and I assumed that he was in the boat accessory business. I was surprised to discover that he was a dentist who practiced four days a week. The other three days he worked his sailboat business. I asked why he was producing sailboat accessories, and he told me that he was looking for something more exciting than dentistry. Dentistry paid most of the bills, but sailing was his love and provided an outlet for his creativity.

How can you identify likely candidates in your area? Unfortunately, since it is very difficult to obtain net worth information about individuals, you may often have to rely on the next-best indicator—income—as a clue to who might have some money to risk. It's true that high income doesn't always mean lots of discretionary cash; people at all income levels may live beyond their means. But using salary as an indicator is the best place to start, provided you keep in mind that you will ultimately be seeking persons with a net worth beyond a salary, home, and car.

Winnowing down these people to a few who have surplus money and are willing to invest it requires using the "quantity principle": For every ten people you solicit, maybe only one or two are in a position to risk some of their cash. And for every ten of those, perhaps only one or two will consider your proposal.

Finding Nearby Angels

People with money to invest move in circles with others who have money. If you're not within those rarified circles, the only way to gain entry is through networking. What does networking mean? It means you're using contacts

for purposes other than the reason you initially made the contact. For example, when your barber says that he knows of a retired executive who might be willing to invest in a startup, or when a local golf pro invites you to join a foursome with a group of investor friends, that's networking. In addition to exploiting these contacts, here are some other sources for finding nearby angels:

- **Professional organizations and other associations.** Organizations for doctors, accountants, dentists, or attorneys are the gathering point for many high-net-worth individuals.
- **Social and sports clubs.** Fraternal organizations, private health clubs, and golf courses are networking sources for potential investors.
- **Seminars and clinics**. Seminars and clinics on financial and business topics attract potential investors.
- **Places of worship**. Many a business deal has been cemented in social gatherings sponsored by churches or synagogues.
- **Service providers**. Your barber, sports trainer, accountant, or computer repair person all may be connected to potential investors.

Once you have a list of prospects—yes, you should maintain a database of potential local investors—you can begin the process of introducing yourself, describing your invention, providing your proposal, and, if desired, presenting your product in action. Be sure to ask each contact, whether receptive or not, for the names of other persons who might be interested in learning about your proposal. (Assure your immediate contact that you will mail your business proposal with a cover letter and not bother the referred person directly). Your contact may prefer to do the mailing. That's fine. Provide a proposal in an envelope with postage already in place. (Yes, there's always a chance that your proposal will be thrown away after you are out of sight but you'll have to take it).

Friends and Relatives

In Chapter 4, I briefly described the process (and risks) of borrowing money from friends and relatives. I also provided some advice on how to borrow money using services such as CircleLending.com (www.Circlelending.com) in Chapter 5. Here, I discuss the concerns you may have when selling an ownership interest in your invention business to friends or relatives.

Friends and relatives who possess surplus savings or income; have money earned from business ventures, inheritance, or profession (as against salary or wages); and have a spirit of adventure and intelligent risk-taking may qualify as an angel.

But be especially conservative when soliciting investments from friends and relatives who do not fit the angel model. If you're serious about preserving friend-

ships and goodwill, avoid soliciting money from persons who invest out of a sense of love or obligation—especially those who seem reluctant to invest but find it difficult or impossible to say no.

Don't let your enthusiasm cloud your sense of sympathy for an investor's financial condition. If in doubt about any friend or relative's capability as an investor, don't even ask. And, as I repeat throughout this book, always inform all investors—especially your nearby angels—that your venture is risky, even if you don't think so.

How Do You Speak to an Angel?

Suppose you do buttonhole someone who has a genuine interest in your invention business. What questions should you ask? The best place to start is by asking what the investor wants to know. Other questions to consider asking: Are you familiar with the industry? What motivates you to invest in a business? What's the best investment you've ever made? Do you invest with others? How long are you willing to wait for a return on your investment?

Keep in mind that angel investing is a personal relationship. That's why it's always better to start your business discussions by learning about the other guy, instead of talking about yourself.

Remote Angels

Your local research may turn up a suitable list of investors, but it may not be enough. It's possible that other investors live within your area, but you will never find out about them. It's easy to understand why these angel investors are hard to locate. You would guard your privacy, too, if you had a net worth over $750,000 and were willing to invest thousands in risky business ventures.

Finding angels outside your personal networks—I call them "remote angels"—requires a different kind of digging. Those are people who may live on the other side of the country, or they may be in your own neighborhood. One characteristic is certain: They are low-profile persons. Another is that they have probably invested in startup businesses before and may presently be involved with one or more startups. In other words, these are more likely to qualify as accredited or professional investors, versus nearby angels, who may have never invested in a venture before. They have money to invest, but they don't advertise it, especially to the typical inventor.

Low profile doesn't mean scarcity, however. According to Jeffrey Sohl, Director of the Center for Venture Research at the University of New Hampshire, hundreds of thousands of angels in the United States invest up to 40 billion dollars annually in over 50,000 companies. This means a rough average of 8,000 angels per state, and an average of 1,000 businesses funded per state. Nearly all of these businesses are in some stage of startup.

Intermediaries: The Good, the Bad, and the Ugly

Before embarking on your search for remote angels, a word about intermediaries—people who, for a fee, promise to bring you investors (sometimes referred to as "matching services"). In every difficult or mysterious aspect of business there are hovering vultures who promise to solve your problems for a fee. Just as invention submission companies that advertise on TV typically bilk inventors out of thousands of dollars, many "money finders" and small business investment brokers often trap unwitting inventors.

Since these money finders and brokers are more legally restricted in their freedom to advertise—because of the securities laws described earlier in this chapter—they mainly depend on you finding them. As Greg Farell wrote in *USA Today*, "... when entrepreneurs venture into this terrain, they are wandering into the Wild West without a horse, a compass, or a gun."

Any person or firm that promises you money without thoroughly examining your business plan, business proposal, or invention idea and holding a personal interview with you, and who wants to charge you a fee, should be suspect. No matter how desperate you are for money, paying large fees (over a thousand dollars) up front is generally an ineffective way for you to try to get money.

"Most [angel brokers] are full of crap," according to Rick LaPierre, an inventor in Lexington, Massachusetts. LaPierre spent an estimated $50,000 on people who promised to introduce him to money people. "They're all nice people, but nothing ever gets done. Everyone they bring in to see you wants another check. It's been a waste of time," says LaPierre.

Here is the dilemma. Most remote angels won't read your proposal unless it comes through referral. That means you will need to find a legitimate angel finder. For inventors, this may be a knowledgeable financial person, such as someone from a SBDC (Small Business Development Center), not a paid broker. But more likely it will be through a legitimate intermediary.

There are two categories of legitimate intermediaries: finders and brokers. Finders become brokers if they charge a percentage of the investment or a fee based on their success in gaining finance. (Brokers may also charge an up-front fee.) A broker, unlike a finder, must be registered with the U.S. Securities & Exchange Commission (SEC).

Finders typically sell lists of potential angels or introduce an inventor to an angel. A broker should do more than that, including matching the inventor and invention with an appropriate angel—a person familiar with the general product of your invention and who has skills needed by the startup. The broker will likely be involved in the negotiations.

How do you to judge the legitimacy of an intermediary? Here are some factors:

- **Watch out for large upfront fees.** The single most important clue is the upfront fee. Such fee, if any, should be low, such as the few hundred dollars that some angel networks charge for "mixers" where inventors meet with angels. When a finder starts talking more than a few hundred dollars, hang up, log off, or walk away. There is no magic threshold except what your own sense tells you is reasonable. But any fees approaching $1,000 start to smell rancid to me. With today's computers it is easy to compile and print out a lot of boilerplate, textbook information, published statistical data, and lists of potential money sources. These may create the illusion that the finder has done a lot of work to justify his existence and his report to you. But be wary. Do your own work, and save the big fees that probably won't get you anything except a headache and substantial debt.

- **Watch out for intermediaries who want to repackage.** Some finders or brokers may want to charge you a large fee to repackage your business plan or write one for you if all you now have is a business proposal. They may suggest that with a better plan you are almost certain to get financed. Again, writing a formal business plan is a task you should learn to do for yourself—most likely in the distant future. (As for business plans, I explain the basics in Chapter 7 and there are many good books on how to create one—for example, Nolo's *How to Write a Business Plan* by Mike McKeever.) For purposes of soliciting angels, your business proposal (as discussed in Chapter 7) should suffice.

- **Watch out for time pressures.** Another sign of illegitimacy in a finder or broker is time pressure. They may tell you that they have an investor who likes your deal, but it must closed within some specific short period of time. This means that you must give them their fee before they'll get you together with the investor. These tactics, of course, are used to get you to act before you wise up. And, somehow, the deal they are so sure will work usually falls through. Remember that investors don't jump into deals. It may take them three to six months or more of investigating you and your claims, and looking at other deals, before they are ready to invest.

- **Be wary of a lack of references.** Another sign of a phony intermediary is a reluctance to furnish references. Actual names of their clients may be hard to get, because many clients don't want their competition to know that they have been financed. But at least a bank, law firm, CPA, or other professional or financial institution should be available as a reference. In any case, ask for client references. A few businesses may surface, especially those that are in the news.

- **Be wary of the red carpet.** Another suspicious sign of an illegitimate intermediary is the "red carpet." A finder or broker who gushes over your invention and your genius is probably a phony. Legitimate brokers know that most inventions never get financed, because they don't show any promise of extraordinary growth and profit. The legitimate finders are conservative in their language and promises.

Can Incubators Help?

Incubators are facilities that generally offer low rent and a variety of services such as management advice and assistance, telephone answering and fax, secretarial, bookkeeping, copying, and possibly reduced-cost professional services. Along with all of these advantages, many incubators will help you to get angel financing. Another innovative option offered by some incubators is group health insurance—a valuable option for the venturer who has lost this benefit after leaving the umbrella of the big corporation.

Incubators will also advise you about sources of funding offered by the federal government, your state or city, if any; help you apply; and possibly act as a referrer.

Most incubators are nonprofit entities and are sponsored by colleges or universities, economic development agencies, local governments, and sometimes a consortium involving two or more of these. Whether nonprofit or for-profit, an incubator must have positive cash flow in order to continue its existence. Fees from rent and services are likely the main source. Many incubators locate in old factory buildings located in low-rent districts in order to keep their costs down. In addition to low rent, some will want a piece of your business or royalties.

One source claims that there are about 1,000 incubators in the U.S. That's an average of 20 per state. To find out more about those in your area, check the National Business Incubation Association (www.nbia.org) or phone your local SBA (Small Business Administration) office, your city's chamber of commerce, your state's general information line, and so forth. Also, search the Internet. Try Google.com using "business incubators" or "(your state) incubators." Whether you sign on or not, your area's incubators may help you find respectable angels. Check them out.

Finding Remote Angels

To give you an idea of the vast collection of resources available, I "Googled" several terms and obtained the following number of listings: "financial angels" (660 listings), "seed money" (171,000 listings), "seed finance" (683 listings), "angel organizations" (170), "angel seminars" (90), "angel groups (31), and "angel clubs" (367). (One tip: Use quotation marks when making similar searches in order to exclude listings for either of the single words by themselves.) Half of these entries have little or nothing to do with finding financial angels. Indeed, many cover the kind of angels with wings. And many other entries are duplicates. So the task of sorting through these resources can be tedious, though not as formidable as it first may appear.

You can find an extensive listing of angel intermediaries, angel investing groups, and individual angels on the Internet. Rather than provide a massive index of potential angel sites, I have provided three sites that can lead you, via links, to everything you'll need. Although I provide these sites, I cannot provide an endorsement for the services provided by various angel groups or investors and advise you to seek professional advice if in doubt about any potential investment.

Active Capital (formerly ACE-NET) (www.activecapital.org) is one of the oldest and most well established sites for entrepreneurs seeking private investment.

Angel Capital Association (www.angelcapitalassociation.org) is the umbrella alliance of many angel groups. Click on "Directory" on the home page for a thorough listing of links to angel groups and resources throughout the U.S.

Cloudstart (www.cloudstart.com) is a private Internet venture finance service that will list your company for a fee (approximately $200 per year). Note, there are other similar services on the Internet.

∎

Chapter 10

Borrowing From the Bank

Will your local bank lend you money for your great idea or an invention? Yes, it will, as long as you can pledge collateral that is worth something more than the amount you wish to borrow. It may even lend a couple of thousand dollars on your signature alone. But it almost certainly won't lend you enough to finance the development, protection, and marketing of your invention without collateral.

Start with this rule about banks: Unless you have assets beyond your great unproved and unprotected idea, you cannot borrow significant sums from a bank. The old saying about bank loans, unfortunately, rings true. It's easier to qualify for a bank loan when you don't need it than when you do. The more speculative that your idea is—that is, the more it requires imagination to envision its success—the less likely you will get a loan. However, the more concrete proof you have of the success—for example, in established sales, an ongoing and successful business, and an experienced, stable business team—the more likely you'll obtain the loan.

Banks—unlike angel investors—don't risk their money. They are *equity lenders*. By that I mean that they will lend you $10,000 if you will put up your home as security, and then only if the equity in your home (net cash realized if it is sold and your mortgage is paid off) exceeds $10,000 by some safe margin that allows for fluctuations in real estate values, the

bank's costs of disposal, and so forth. (For more information on signature loans, credit card loans, and predatory lending practices, read Chapter 4.)

Not only that, but getting bank loans for your small business has gotten progressively harder in the past two decades. Why? According to a study by University of Houston professors Steven C. Craig and Pauline Hardee, loan approval is often based on a personal relationship. This is especially true in cases where the business's total debt exceeds its assets.

Unfortunately, in these days of mega-bank mergers, the personal relationship (between bank officers and business owners) is disappearing. Craig and Hardee reported that small business owners were 25% less likely to get loan approvals in regions dominated by large banks (those with more than $5 billion in assets) than in areas with lots of smaller lenders.

For the inventor-for-royalties who wants to license an invention, a small signature-size loan ($10,000 or less) may be sufficient, as it could pay for the costs of prototyping and patenting the invention. But for the entrepreneurial inventor, the amounts available from a bank (without mortgaging everything you own) will not be sufficient.

Isn't your invention worth a lot of money, and won't a bank consider it as reasonable assurance of repayment? Not a chance. Your patent may be worth a million dollars to you, but to the bank it is just mysterious pieces of paper, and its value is only credible when it is the instrument that helps to ensure predictable and profitable cash flow from the sale of a product, and the cash is actually flowing. Even then, a patent is an asset of uncertain value until it has been challenged in court and the court declares in favor of the inventor.

The bank will want your home (not your patent) as security, not only because it is worth a definite amount of money, but also because banks understand how to dispose of homes and recover their money in cases of default. They likely wouldn't have the foggiest idea of what to do with your patent if you defaulted.

If this still doesn't seem right to you, perhaps it will help you to consider the five "C's" of credit—the formula upon which lenders consistently rely when deciding to make loans.

Types of Financial Institution Loans

Not all bank loans are the same. Below are some of the common types of loans offered by financial institutions.

Signature loans. These are small loans available from your bank based on your credit rating and your history with the bank. (The name refers to the fact that all that is required is the consumer's signature to make it binding.) If your credit history is good, you can often get a few thousand dollars without pledging collateral. (For more on signature loans, review Chapter 4.)

Lines of credit. Lines of credit are loans commonly used in cash-flow crunches—for example, you owe suppliers and employees but haven't received income from sales. Generally, interest on a line of credit is paid monthly, and the principal can be demanded at any time (referred to as "demand loans"). Sometimes the line of credit is temporary—for example, for temporary projects—and sometimes it lasts up to 36 months, after which the line of credit becomes a term loan (see below). Lenders rarely provide revolving credit to a new business—that is, one lacking any history of sales or revenue.

Term loans. These are your typical loans that are made for a period of years and require regular payments of principal and interest based upon an amortization schedule.

Swing loans. Sometimes called "bridge loans," these are commonly used when businesses need money to close a deal, usually over the concurrent purchase and sale of real estate.

The Sixth "C"— Credit Risk Modeling

The five "C's" of credit, described below, may soon be replaced by a mathematic standard known as credit risk modeling (CRM). Based on the work of Nobel laureate Robert Merton, CRM uses software program models that attempt to predict when a firm's assets will fall below liabilities. CRMs can look at financial ratios and historic records of defaulting business and predict— based on your finances—whether your venture will succeed or fail (and when). Though currently only in use by a few of the top banks, you can expect that this methodology will eventually trickle down for use in many loan decisions.

The Five "C's" of Credit

To ensure that a bank gets paid back, it usually considers the following five factors:

- **Capacity.** Some finance experts consider capacity to repay to be the most critical of the five factors. Capacity refers to how you intend to repay the loan—that is, from where will the loan payments come? The bank expects these payments will come from an operating business—not a plan for a future enterprise. So, if you haven't commenced business, that's one strike against you when seeking a loan. The lender considers the cash flow from the business, the timing of the repayment, and the probability of successful repayment of the loan. The bank also looks at the payment history on existing credit relationships—personal and commercial—which are considered an indicator of future payment performance. What bankers like to see is slow, consistent growth and that profits are retained within the business. Again, without any history or ongoing business, you are likely to flunk this factor. Prospective lenders also will want to know about your contingent sources of repayment.

- **Capital.** Capital is the money you personally have invested in the business and is an indication of how much you have at risk should the business fail. As I stressed in Chapter 4, prospective lenders and investors will expect you to have contributed from your own assets and to have undertaken personal financial risk to establish the business before asking them to commit any funding. Banks believe that if you have a significant personal investment in the business you are more likely to do everything in your power to make the business successful (and less likely to default on the loan).

- **Collateral.** Collateral or "guarantees" are the additional forms of security you can provide the lender. If for some reason the business cannot repay its bank loan, the bank wants to know there is a second source of repayment. Assets such as your home, business equipment, buildings, accounts receivable, and, in some cases, inventory are considered possible sources of repayment if they are sold by the bank for cash. Both business and personal assets can be sources of collateral for a loan. Collateral is different from a guarantee—when someone else signs a guarantee document promising to repay the loan if you can't. Some lenders may require such a guarantee in addition to collateral as security for a loan.

- **Conditions.** Conditions focus on the intended purpose of the loan. Will the money be used for working capital, additional equipment, or inventory? Here again, the inventor is at a disadvantage, since the purpose of the loan is—from the bank's perspective—incredibly speculative. The bank may also consider the economic climate and conditions, both within the industry of your invention and in other industries that could affect your business.

- **Character.** Some lenders may give this factor more weight than others. Character is the general impression you make on the potential lender or investor. The bank's loan officer will form a subjective opinion as to whether or not you are sufficiently trustworthy to repay the loan or generate a return on funds invested in your company. (You should expect, of course, that the bank will run credit checks and other background checks to confirm personal findings.) Again, if you have no experience in industry—even if you are a genius in your field of invention—you may have a serious disadvantage. The quality of your references and the background and experience of your employees also will be taken into consideration.

Of course, these five factors are really pointing to the same basic question: Is there hard evidence that you can repay the loan? So, how does the entrepreneurial inventor qualify for a loan from the local bank without pledging his home or other traditional assets?

The only possibility, unfortunately, is if you are an established business and you can meet the typical criteria. In other words, if you want a loan of $100,000 or more, you will need to have an operating business with substantial cash flow from sales of your invention product. Obviously, if you're at that point, you may wonder why you need a bank loan in the first place.

SBA Loans

The federal government has systems (as do some states) for fostering business startups and the introduction of new products. The Departments of Commerce understand the difficulties faced by new entrepreneurs, and they believe that it is their duty to keep our economy growing through business startups, among other things. One federal agency supporting that principle is the SBA (Small Business Administration), which backs bank loans. The SBA does not make loans; it guarantees loans. So, you will still be dealing with your local bank. The SBA's mandate is to entice banks to make business loans by guaranteeing up to 85% of the loan amount in the event of default. According to the National Association of Government Guaranteed Lenders, a trade group, the SBA guaranteed 67,306 loans totaling $11.3 billion in the fiscal year that ended in September 2004.

In order to qualify for an SBA loan, your business must be organized as a for-profit entity and must be independently owned and operated. (The SBA does not make loans to companies that are dominant within their industry). There are also limits as to how many employees and sales you must have, depending on the type of business seeking the loan.

The SBA has several loan programs and similar services. Below are some of the well-known programs:

- **The 7(a) program.** The 7(a) is usually the first choice for startups or companies in their early phases. The average 7(a) loan is approximately $240,000. 7(a) loans cannot exceed $750,000, and interest can be fixed or variable. Although you're not required to make an investment in your business, lenders prefer to see an owner contribution in the business of at least 20% to 30%. Despite the SBA support, lenders usually require 100% collateral for the loan as well as guarantees from all business owners with more than 20% interest. 7(a) loans have become more accessible for some business since the SBA introduced a new "low-doc" system that requires less documentation.
- **The 504 program.** The 504 program is for growing businesses that are looking to expand. These are substantial loans (an average of over $300,000) for major projects such as financing real estate or equipment purchases and require collateralization and personal guarantees.
- **The 7(m) Microloan Loan program.** The 7(m) Microloan Loan program provides short-term loans of up to $35,000 to small businesses and non-profit childcare centers for working capital or the purchase of inventory, supplies, furniture, fixtures, machinery, and/or equipment. Proceeds cannot be used to pay existing debts or to

purchase real estate. The 7(m) loans are not guaranteed by the SBA and are only available in selected locations in most states.

- **SBA prequalification program.** The SBA has a loan prequalification program which may be of interest to inventors who are low-income borrowers, disabled business owners, new and emerging businesses, veterans, exporters, and rural and specialized industries. These designated small business applicants can have their loan applications for $250,000 or less analyzed and potentially sanctioned by an SBA "intermediary" before they are taken to lenders for consideration. The SBA intermediary organizations assist prospective borrowers in developing viable loan application packages and securing loans. For more on these loan opportunities, check the SBA website (www.sba.gov). Click "Financing Your Business" and review "SBA Loan Programs."

That said, be prepared for the same advice as in the previous section—that is, without an ongoing (and financially promising) business, you're unlikely to qualify for SBA assistance. If you are interested in pursuing the SBA or your state's equivalent department, verify the general requirements for loans as posted at the SBA website (www.sba.gov).

For loans under $100,000, the SBA does not require a business plan. The bank's application alone is sufficient. In other words, the SBA's policy is that below some dollar level they accept the bank's investigation and assessment of risk. Above that dollar level the SBA wants to form its own opinion of the risk of granting your loan.

If you are seeking an SBA loan, by staying below this threshold dollar amount you will be able to deal only with your local bank, and your chances of forming a more personal relationship with a lending officer are much higher than in dealing "at arm's length" with the SBA by way of pieces of paper. A personal relationship doesn't mean that a loan officer will approve your application merely because you have a nice smile. But you will have a chance to present odds and ends of information that may not be in your business plan but which will help sway the decision.

In addition, always remember the business realities associated with SBA-guaranteed bank loans. The SBA only guarantees 85 percent of the loan. In other words, the bank will usually take a hit of 15 percent of the unpaid loan balance if you default on payback.

The SBA provides others services, the most popular of which is the SCORE program (the Service Corps of Retired Executives). SCORE, a group of volunteers, can be a very valuable ally along the way. Some inventors swear by its assistance, but a few have told me that the executive advising them was not sufficiently experienced in the kind of help they needed. If that is the problem in your case, simply ask for another SCORE adviser. This problem can largely be avoided by thinking through your needs ahead of time and explaining them in detail to the SCORE liaison.

Even more helpful than SCORE, because their services are more comprehensive, are the Small Business Development Centers (SBDCs). SBDCs are a consortium of the federal government's Small Business Administration, a state university, and private enterprise. The SBDC services, which include help with writing your business plan, one-on-one counseling, workshops, databases, and many, many other accommodations, are free. You can locate one near you by entering "SBDC plus [your state]" on a good search engine, such as Google.

My goal in discussing bank loans is not to be discouraging. They can be acquired, and they may be essential to your success. But you will be getting them on the bank's terms, not yours. So even though the loan officer thinks you are wonderful, there is still a bit of unemotional assessment by committee going on after you leave the bank.

One last point on banks: All banks are vitally concerned about their ROA (return on assets). "Return" is simply the money left over from income after paying all expenses. And assets are the moneys on deposit, plus real estate and other tangibles that the bank may hold. ROA is just a more exacting way of saying profit. If a bank's ROA is shaky, it is less likely to take risks than if it is making a healthy ROA. That's logical. So, look at the financial reports of several banks in your area and compare them. Banks are obliged by regulation to disclose this information, and all banks will have available a printed "Statement of Condition." This information is also available through the Federal Deposit Insurance Corporation (www.fdic.gov), a government function that guarantees your deposits.

States Business Development Offices

In addition to federal promotion of small business through the SBA, some states promote small business. Connecticut, where I live, has a program similar to the SBAs known as the Connecticut Development Authority. Your state will likely have an equivalent department. Look in the blue page government listing section of your phone book for similar state agencies. If you're unsure, inquire at your secretary of state's office. If there is such an office, visit the agency and talk with someone who will listen to your plans and advise you as to when that agency will be willing to help you make your plans a reality.

Beyond Angels

In previous chapters I discussed common methods for financing your invention idea or preparing for the licensing of an invention product. In this chapter I briefly discuss:

- venture capitalists (VCs), and
- exits strategies—for example, initial public offerings (IPOs), sales, and mergers

I provide only a brief discussion of exit strategies and VCs, because these activities require assistance beyond the scope of this book (and are the subject of books, themselves).

Venture Capitalists

Like angels, venture capitalists (VCs) want to use your great idea in order to make money, lots of money. The venture capitalist is an institutionalized version of the angel investor, except with access to a lot more cash. VCs are the big leagues of the investment world—tapping into the elite of financing such as investment bankers, mutual fund owners, and so forth.

Venture capital investors differ from angel investors in a few key ways. Angels invest their own money in ventures; VCs invest money acquired from financial institutions and wealthy individuals. Angels don't have to invest. They can put their money in the bank if they wish. VCs have to invest in order to earn profits for their investors. Angels typically invest from $25,000 to $250,000; VCs typically

invest a minimum of three to five million dollars.

VCs are exceptionally discerning, choosing to invest in fewer than 2% of the proposals that come their way. When they do invest, it's usually because they determine there is a very experienced management team, an untapped niche, and a chance for remarkable returns. They expect a minimum return of 40% annually on their investment.

VCs judge the management team as the most essential of the elements comprising your enterprise. Your invention is secondary. This means that you will come under intense scrutiny for your ability to perform a vital role in your business. If you have acted as the CEO (Chief Executive Officer) from the beginning, you will likely have to concede this role to someone who is more qualified if you expect to receive VC funding.

Landing VC funding is a very long shot for most businesses. Getting access to VCs is largely a matter of being referred rather than going in through the mailroom. VC funding can also be unforgiving—for example, if you lose a key member of the management team, or if the technology on which the product is based changes unexpectedly, the VCs may pull the plug on your venture and accept the loss.

You can find more information about venture capital funding at the National venture Capital Association (www.nvca .com).

Exit Strategies: IPOs, Mergers and Sales

Investors usually expect a 20% to 50% annual return, and they expect to earn it within three to five years. Since it's unlikely they will receive this compensation solely from the sale of your invention product—that revenue is commonly needed to pay your ongoing expenses—investors employ a few common strategies for recouping their investment (known as "exit strategies"). The most common exit strategies are:

- IPOS—offering stock to the public
- sale of the company, or merger with another company.

Less-common strategies include a buyout, in which one shareholder buys out the others, and franchising, in which the basic business model is sold over and over to franchisees.

Going Public (the IPO)

An IPO is the sale of stock to the public for the purposes of raising cash to expand your business. The process is expensive—anywhere from $250,000 to $1,000,000—and it is always a gamble, because there is no assurance that the public will buy the stock that you're offering.

Unlike the selling of stock in a small corporation, selling to the public (meaning investors whom you don't know and will probably never meet) is strictly regulated by the Securities and Exchange Commission. Details of IPO strategies and mechanism are well beyond the scope of this book. If you get to the lofty heights where an IPO seems doable, you will also be able to pay for the hundreds of thousands of dollars' worth of professional advice needed.

Merger or Sale

Another common exit strategy option—more common than sale of stock to the public—is the merger with, or sale of the business to, another corporation. In either event your stock value is multiplied by a variable that is based on your projected sales and growth. So, if your sales are leveling off due to changes inherent in the marketplace, your chances for a large gain on your investment are low.

When you read about mergers or sales of companies to larger corporations, the deals always involve large sums of money, often in the billions of dollars. However, most sales or mergers of companies are much smaller, in the hundreds of thousands of dollars or, perhaps, low millions.

If you are seeking to merge or sell to a larger corporation, consider approaching a company that has a line of products in which yours will fit, and ask for financial sponsorship. This doesn't mean approaching a mousetrap manufacturer if you have invented a better mousetrap. Why should they want to compete with themselves by introducing another mousetrap? Instead, approach a manufacturer of rat poison, which can market a better mousetrap through its existing marketing channels.

Final Thoughts

As you consider your quest for financing and before you spend any significant amount of money on your venture (on a patent, for example), think through what is it that you hope to accomplish. How far are you willing to go? What will be the end of your quest? Do you want to grow old with an interesting and profitable business based on your invention or great idea? Do you want to witness enough great growth such that the public demands your product and you can sell out to large corporation?

However you think about the end of your participation in your venture, you must crystallize your thoughts before you take on early investors and angels. Before

you ask for money, always consider how you will be paying it back. Your friends and relatives may be relaxed about how and when they will get their money back, but the higher you go up the investment ladder, the less tolerant the investors will be of any vagueness regarding your end goal.

As you are aware from reading this book, the burden of finding and convincing the right investor that your great idea or invention is the right one is a difficult, challenging task. You must believe passionately in your dream and communicate your vision clearly. And, most important, to paraphrase author Richard Stein (*Crossing the Swamp*), you must be "failure-tolerant."

I hope this books helps. If you have any suggestions or changes, or just want to pass along a success story, please email me at jack@inventor-mentor.com.

■

Chapter 12

Resources

Thidrawis chapter provides various resources that can help you in your pursuit of growth, invention protection, and financing. I cannot provide blanket endorsements for these resources, nor can I vouch for the accuracy of the information provided by these sources. However, in general, I've found these listing to be helpful and informative and suggest that you review them.

Magazines

- *Inventors' Digest* (www.inventors digest.com) is the only North American magazine solely for inventors. Subscription Dept. 1-800-838-8808.
- *Inc.* (www.inc.com) provides information for small businesses and startups.

Software

- *Business Plan Pro* (Palo Alto Software) provides the most comprehensive business plan creation software.
- *Patent Pending Now* (Nolo) provides all you need to prepare a provisional patent application.
- *PatentEase* (Inventorprise, Inc.) is an interactive program that assists in preparing patent applications and allows for importing of patent drawings.

Books

- *Angel Financing: How to Find and Invest in Private Equity* (Wiley), by Benjamin and Margulis
- *Angel Investing: Matching Start-Up Funds With Start-up Companies* (Jossey-Bass), by Osnabrugee and Robinson
- *Burn Your Business Plan!: What Investors Really Want From Entrepreneurs*, (Lauson Publishing), by David Gumpert
- *Design for Manufacturability Handbook* (McGraw Hill Professional), by James G. Bralla
- *Entrepreneur Magazine: Bringing Your Product to Market* (Wiley), by Don Debelak
- *Form Your Own Limited Liability Company* (Nolo), by Anthony Mancuso
- *How to Make Patent Drawings Yourself*, (Nolo), by Jack Lo and David Pressman
- *How to Market a Product for Under $500!: A Handbook of Multiple Exposure Marketing* (Danielle Adams), by Dobkin and Axelrod
- *Incorporate Your Business: A 50-State Legal Guide to Forming a Corporation* (Nolo), by Anthony Mancuso
- *What Every Inventor Needs to Know about Law and Taxes,* (Nolo) by Stephen Fishman
- *License Your Invention* (Nolo), by Richard Stim

- *LLC or Corporation?: How to Choose the Right Form for Your Business* (Nolo) by Anthony Mancuso
- *Millions from the Mind: How To Turn Your Invention—Or Someone Else's—Into a Fortune* (James White & Assoc.), by Alan R. Tripp
- *Nolo's Patents for Beginners* (Nolo), by David Pressman and Richard Stim
- *Nondisclosure Agreements: Protect Your Trade Secrets & More* (Nolo), by Richard Stim and Stephen Fishman
- *Patent It Yourself* (Nolo), by David Pressman
- *Patent Pending in 24 Hours* (Nolo) by Richard Stim and David Pressman
- *Patent, Copyright, & Trademark: An Intellectual Property Desk Reference* (Nolo), by Richard Stim
- *Stand Alone, Inventor!: And Make Money With Your New Product Ideas* (Lee Publishing), by Robert G. Merrick
- *The Inventor's Notebook* (Nolo), by Fred Grissom and David Pressman
- *The Small Business Advisor* (Wiley), by Entrepreneur Magazine
- *Trademark: Legal Care for Your Business & Product Name* (Nolo), by Stephen Elias
- *Uncommon Marketing Techniques* (Danielle Adams), by Dobkin and Axelrod
- *Will It Sell?,* by James E. White. Excellent for invention self-evaluation.

Inventor Resources

Here is a collection various resources that you may find useful for marketing or financing your invention.

- Accessory Brainstorms (www. accessorybrainstorms.com) offers services particularly for fashion-related inventors.
- Ask the Inventors (www.askthe inventors.com). The Ghostline Gals, two successful women inventors, help other inventors to success.
- Books for Inventors (www.Books ForInventors.com) has—you guessed it—helpful books for inventors.
- EGT Global Trading (www.home-town.aol.com/egtglobaltrading) provides overseas production of sewn items, fashions, baby access., household inventions, and so forth.
- Google Catalogs (http://catalogs. google.com) provides a categorical listing of catalog houses.
- Harvey Reese Associates/Money4 Ideas.com (www.money4ideas.com) is the website of Harvey Reese, author of *Licensing Your Invention,* and offers marketing, licensing, and product development.
- Idea Rights.com (www.idearights. com) is Jim White's dose of reality for inventors. And for more from Jim, check out "Will It Sell?" (www .willitsell.com/patmyths.htm)
- WIN Innovation Institute (www .innovation-institute.com) provides

product evaluations and is affiliated with Southwest Missouri State University (SMSU).

- Internet Patent News Service (www.bustpatents.com) is a source for patent news, information about searching, and patent documents.
- InventNet Forum (www.inventnet.com) provides an online forum and mailing list if you wish to contact other inventors.
- Inventor Mentor (www.inventor-mentor.com). My website for mentoring inventors.
- Intellectual Property Owners (Ipo) (www.ipo.org) sponsors the National Inventor of the Year Award and serves owners of patents, trademarks, copyrights, and trade secrets.
- Jobshop (www.jobshop.net) helps buyers of custom contract manufactured parts.
- Market Launchers (www.Market-Launchers.com) lists inventions for sale.
- Minnesota Inventors Congress (www.invent1.org) is one of the oldest and most respected inventor organizations.
- National Business Incubation Association (www.nbia.org) is a grouping of incubator facilities throughout the nation.
- National Technology Transfer Center (NTTC) (www.nttc.edu) helps entrepreneurs and companies looking to access federally funded research and development activity at U.S. universities.
- Patent Info (www.uspatentinfo.com) provides patent information and resources.
- Patent Law Links (www.patentlawlinks.com) provides links to everything "patent" on the Internet.
- Product Solutions, International (www.ProductSolutionsIntl.com) offers manufacturing services.
- Ronald J. Riley's Inventor Resources (www.inventored.org) offers a set of comprehensive links and advice for inventors.
- TG Ideas (http://my.athenet.net/~ideas/) circulates a newsletter of ideas for products and services.
- The Patent Café (www.patentcafe.com) is a comprehensive site for information and services on invention development, protection, licensing, and manufacturing.
- United Inventors Association (www.UIAUSA.org) is a nonprofit inventor organization.
- Wisconsin Innovation Center (http://academics.uww.edu/business/innovate) offers invention evaluation, partnership, and a wide range of services.
- Workshop Publishing (www.build-stuff.com) has plans, books, and videos on plastic casting, building machines for vacuum forming, plastic injection molding, and so forth.

Patent Law and Intellectual Property Law Websites

- Copyright Office (www.copyright. gov) has numerous circulars, kits, and other publications that can help you, including one on searching copyright records.
- European Patent Office (Epo) (www.european-patent-office.org) is the agency that implements the European Patent Convention—a simplified method of acquiring a patent among member nations.
- Fedlaw (www.thecre.com/fedlaw/ default.htm) is a source of federal law links with a thorough collection of intellectual property statutes, case law, and readings.
- Patent & Trademark Office (PTO) (www.uspto.gov) offers a number of informational pamphlets, including an introduction to patents ("General Information About Patents") and an alphabetical and geographical listing of patent attorneys and agents registered to practice before the PTO ("Directory of Registered Patent Attorneys and Agents Arranged by States and Countries"). Most patent forms can be downloaded from the PTO website, as can many important publications including the Manual of Patent Examining Procedures, Examination Guidelines for Computer-Related Inventions, and Disclosure Document Program.

- PCT Applicant's Guide (www.wipo. int) provides PCT information and software for facilitating completion of the PCT forms is available through the PCT's website.
- Trade Secrets Home Page (www .execpc.com/~mhallign) has explanations of trade secret law online and current trade secret news.
- Trademark Office (www.uspto.gov) provides information about trademarks examination and registration.

Patent Searching

Here are several organizations that offer computer searching of patent records and a description of their services. Several of the "for fee" databases also provide foreign patent information.

- Delphion (www.delphion.com) provides fee-based online searchable database with full text searching capability for patents issued from 1974 to the present.
- Foreign Patent Searching (http:// patent.search-in.net) has information on searching foreign patents.
- LexPat (www.lexis-nexis.com) is a commercial database of U.S. patents searchable from 1971 to the present. In addition, the LEXPAT library offers extensive prior art searching capability of technical journals and magazines.
- MicroPatent (www.micropatent. com) is a commercial database of

U.S. patents searchable from 1836 to the present. Users must first set up an account. It also offers delivery of patent copies dating back to 1790 by U.S. mail, fax, and email.

• QPAT (www.qpat.com) and Questel/Orbit (www.questel.orbit.com) are both commercial services that access the QPAT database, which includes U.S. patents searchable from 1974 to the present and full-text European A (1987-present) and B (1991-present) patents.

• U.S. Patent & Trademark Office (www.uspto.gov) offers a free online full-text searchable database of patents and drawings that covers the period from January 1976 to the most recent weekly issue date (usually each Tuesday). In order to view the drawings, your computer must be able to view TIFF files. The PTO's site is linked to a source that provides a free downloadable TIFF reader program. For faster searching, there is also a Bibliographic Database that contains only the text of each patent without drawings.

Patent Searchers

Here are some patent searching services. You can find many more using Google or the patent links and resources listed above.

• Patent Search International (www.patentsearchinternational.com). Ron Brown guarantees that if the patent examiner rejects your application based on a patent the Brown failed to find, your search fee will be refunded.

• Intellectual Asset Management Group (Dgrantk@aol.com) provides patentability searches.

• Affiliated Inventors Foundation, Inc. (www.affiliatedinventors.com) offers patent searches and patentability opinions.

Nolo's Legal Encyclopedia

Nolo's website (www.nolo.com) features an extensive Legal Encyclopedia that includes a section on intellectual property. You'll find answers to frequently asked questions about patents, copyrights, trademarks, and other related topics, as well as sample chapters of Nolo books and a wide range of articles. Simply click on "Legal Encyclopedia" and then on "Patents, Copyright, & Trademark."

Nonprofit Inventor Associations

Here are some of my favorite inventor organizations:

- InventNet Forum (www.inventnet. com) provides an online forum and mailing list if you wish to contact other inventors.
- Minnesota Inventors Congress (www.invent1.org) is one of the oldest and most respected inventor organizations.
- United Inventors Association (www. uiausa.org) is the umbrella organization for inventor groups in the U.S. and Canada and also helps individual inventors not presently served by a local inventor group.

Invention and Related Trade Shows

Below is a brief sample of invention and related trade shows. For a complete offering of trade shows, perform a Google search such as "trade shows." (Be sure to use quotes.).

- AAPEX (www.aapexshow.com) is the trade show for the Automotive Aftermarket Products Expo. 708-226-1300.
- Home Idea Show (www.homeidea-show.com) is the source for home improvement products.
- Innoventions Show (www.home-show.net/innovent) is a Toronto-based invention showcase.

- Minnesota Inventors Congress (www.invent1.org) has an annual exposition and seminars in mid-June.
- Variety Merchandise Show (www. merchandisegroup.com) exhibits a wide range of merchandise inventions.
- Yankee Invention Exposition and Yankee Entrepreneur Workshops (www.yankeeinventionexpo.com) showcases an annual exposition of inventions (mid-October) in Waterbury, Connecticut that draws inventors from around the world.

Design and Prototyping Services

You can find many prototype and design services on the web. Below are a few that I've uncovered.

- America Invents Prototyping (www. AmericaInvents.com) does product development, marketing, and licensing.
- Art.Tec (www.arttec.net) offers electronic prototype services.
- Bob "Mac" McIlvaine (603-673-5861) provides electronic and mechanical design, embedded processors, and CAD presentation packages.
- Bob DeWitty (bobdewitty@chemical prototype.net) provides prototyping of chemical-based inventions.
- CDS Worldwide (www.cdsworld wide.com) provides prototyping,

engineering, tooling, and package design

- Development Technologies (www. development-technologies.com) offers prototyping, design, tooling, and cold casting of urethane.
- Electromechanica (www.engineeringprototypes.com) offers design and prototyping services.
- Engineering F/X (www.engineeringfx.com) provides prototyping, design, and drafting services.
- Frank Mold Design, Inc. (FMDinc@aol.com) provides design and prototype services.
- Hebert Engineering & Design Co. (www.engineeringprototypes.com) offers design services.
- Herb Ross Brown (Hbrown40@webtv.net) does prototyping, tooling, and molding.
- Kaiser Technology Co., Ltd. (Claire@kaiser-tech.com.tw) does prototyping, CAD engineering design, tooling, molding, and printing.
- Industrial Designers Society of America (www.idsa.org) is a directory of U.S. designers and often posts member credentials or job searches.
- Obvia (skeeley@attbi.com) does virtual prototyping, physical prototyping, 3D renderings, and illustrations.
- Retronix (www.retronix.biz) does prototyping and engineering assistance.

- Sterling Group (203-982-4999) does product design on 3D CAD.
- Zigounakis Custom Fabrication (415-669-7837) does prototyping, design, and development.

Marketing, Licensing, and Rep Services

Here are some services that may be able to rep or assist you with marketing of your invention product.

- America Invents (www.America Invents.com) provides marketing, licensing, and product development.
- Doug Comstock (Doug@TheMarketingGuru.com) is a presentation skills coach and publicist.
- Dr. Doug Brown (drdbrown@att. net) helps with pre- and post-launch services including research, development, strategy, licensing, and joint venturing.
- Excel Development Group, Inc. (www.exceld.com) specializes in toy and game licensing.
- Innovative Consulting Group (www.biz-consult.com) does test marketing, product launches, and focus groups.
- MarketLaunchers (www.Market-Launchers.com) provides web advertising for inventors.
- Mary Ellroy (gamebird@compuserve. com) consults with toy and game inventors.

- Mike Marks (mikemarks@capecod. net) a respected consultant on tools and related items.
- New Concept Advisors (www .newconceptadvisors.com) offers consulting services.
- Patent License Exchanges such as Yet2.com (www.yet2.com), the Patent and License Exchange (www.pl-x.com), 2XFR.com (www.2xfr.com), and NewIdeaTrade. com (www.newideatrade.com) offer—for a fee—the ability to post information about patented inventions for would-be licensees.
- Pelham West Associates (www .pelhamwest.com) scouts and consults for new products.
- Scott Keeley (s.keeley@attbi.com) specializes in tools and toys.
- Solve-It Marketing Company (www. solve-itmarketing.com) does warehousing, shipping and receiving, accounting, invoicing, and collection.
- Synchronicity (www.synclicensing .com) provides marketing and licensing services.
- Tillberry Direct Marketing (www. catalogrep.com) represents products to the catalog industry.
- Ultra-Search, Inc. (714-779-0151) does research on ideas, products, technologies, and processes.
- VentureABC.com (www.venture-ABC.com) provides a worldwide invention directory.

Manufacturing Services

- Jim Richardson, Richardson Associates. Contract manufacturing management, sourcing from prototype to production (especially plastic injection-molded products). www.richardson-assoc.com.
- Jobshop.com (www.jobshop.com) provides a nationwide directory of manufacturing sources
- Product Solutions International, Inc. (www.ProductSolutionsIntl.com) does development and manufacturing of invention/products.
- Pacific Source, Inc. (www.pacific-source-inc.com) does engineering and prototyping assistance for manufacturing in China.
- Darleen Flaig (508-261-9153) is a pre-manufacturing and manufacturing liaison.
- The Better Mousetrap People (www.thetrap.com) provide design, sourcing, offshore production, packaging, and other services.
- SIC codes can be found at the North American Industry Classification System website (www.naics.com).
- Thomas Register, available online (www.thomasregister.com) or in print format, *Thomas Register of American Manufacturers* (Thomas Register Publishing). The Thomas Register lists manufacturers by subject and provides profiles and phone numbers.

Mentoring Services

- Jack Lander (www.inventor-mentor. com) (author of this book) person- ally coaches inventors. Money-back guarantee. You like it or you don't pay
- The Ghostline Gals (www .asktheinventors.com). Mary Sarao and Barbara Pitts, successful Texas inventors.

Finding and Using a Lawyer

An experienced attorney may help answer your invention and business questions and allay your fears about pro- tecting your invention and setting up and running your business. Below we have divided attorneys into two groups: inven- tor attorneys that can help in the protec- tion and licensing of your invention, and business attorneys that can help in set- ting up and running your business.

Inventor Attorneys

The best way to get a referral to a good patent lawyer is to talk to other people who have actually used a particular lawyer's services. *Inventors' Digest* is also an excellent source (see listing in this chapter). The worst way is to comb through advertisements or unscreened lists of lawyers provided by a local bar association or the phone company. Also avoid yellow page listings that are cap- tioned "patenting services." These listings are often marketing scams that mislead inventors

In general, there are two groups of inventor attorneys: those who are licensed to practice before the USPTO (patent attorneys), and those who are not. You should consult a patent attorney for assistance performing pat- ent searching, drafting a provisional or regular patent application, responding to patent examiners, and dealing with the USPTO. An attorney does not have to be licensed to practice before the USPTO in order to enforce your patent in a court case. We recommend that you use a patent attorney to prepare or analyze patent-related agreements on your behalf—for example, to prepare in- vention assignments, license agreements, or co-inventorship agreements. That said, many attorneys who are not licensed to practice before the USPTO can negotiate, prepare, and enforce license agreements and ventures. Patent and intellectual property attorneys generally charge $200 to $400 per hour, and a full-blown patent lawsuit can run to hundreds or even thousands of hours' work before it even goes to trial.

Business and Tax Attorneys

There are many attorneys who specialize in advising small businesses. These lawyers are a bit like general practitio- ner doctors: They know a little about a lot of different areas of law. A lawyer with plenty of experience working with businesses should be able to answer your basic inventor business questions.

Such a lawyer can help you:

- start your business—review incorporation documents, for example, analyze zoning ordinances, land use regulations, and private title documents that may restrict your ability to work at home
- review contractor agreements
- assess how and when to transfer equity in your business
- coach or represent you in lawsuits or arbitrations where the stakes are high or the legal issues complex
- deal with intellectual property issues—copyrights, trademarks, patents, trade secrets, and business names, or
- look over a proposed office lease.

Finding a Business Lawyer

The best way to locate a small business lawyer is through referrals from other self-employed people in your community. Industry associations and trade groups are also excellent sources of referrals. If you already have or know a lawyer, he or she might also be able to refer you to an experienced person who has the qualifications you need. Other people, such as your banker, accountant, or insurance agent, may know of good business lawyers.

Local bar associations often maintain and advertise lawyer referral services. However, a lawyer can usually get on this list simply by volunteering. Very little (if any) screening is done to find out whether the lawyers are any good. Similarly, advertisements in the yellow pages, in newspapers, on television, or online say nothing meaningful about a lawyer's skills or manner—just that he could afford to pay for the ad. In many states, lawyers can advertise any specialization they choose—even if they have never handled a case in that area of law.

Paying a Lawyer

Whenever you hire a lawyer, insist upon a written explanation of how the fees and costs will be paid.

Most business lawyers charge by the hour. Hourly rates vary, but in most parts of the United States, you can get competent services for your business for $150 to $250 an hour. Comparison shopping among lawyers will help you avoid overpaying. But the cheapest hourly rate isn't necessarily the best. A novice who charges only $80 an hour may take three hours to review a consulting contract. A more experienced lawyer who charges $200 an hour may do the same job in half an hour and make better suggestions. If a lawyer will be delegating some of the work on your case to a less-experienced associate, paralegal, or secretary, that work should be billed at a lower hourly rate. Be sure to get this information recorded in your initial written fee agreement.

Sometimes, a lawyer may quote you a flat fee for a specific job. For example, a lawyer may offer to incorporate your business for a flat fee of $2,000. You pay the same amount regardless of how much time the lawyer spends. This can be cheaper than paying an hourly fee, but not always.

Alternatively, some self-employed people hire lawyers on retainer—that is, they pay a flat annual fee in return for the lawyer handling all their routine legal business. However, few small businesses can afford to keep a lawyer on retainer.

Using a Lawyer as a Legal Coach

One way to keep your legal costs down is to do as much work as possible yourself and simply use the lawyer as your coach. For example, you can draft your own agreements, giving your lawyer the relatively quick and inexpensive task of reviewing them. But get a clear understanding about who's going to do what. You don't want to do the work and get billed for it because the lawyer duplicated your efforts. And you certainly don't want any crucial elements to fall through cracks because you each thought the other person was attending to the work.

Help From Other Experts

Lawyers aren't the only ones who can help you deal with the legal issues involved in financing your invention. Tax professionals, members of trade groups, and the Small Business Administration can also be very helpful.

Tax Professionals

Tax professionals include tax attorneys, certified public accountants, and enrolled agents. Tax pros can answer your tax questions and help you with tax planning, preparing your tax returns, and dealing with IRS audits.

Industry and Trade Associations

Business or industry trade associations or similar organizations can be useful sources of information and services. Many such groups track federal and state laws, lobby Congress and state legislatures, and even help members deal with the IRS and other federal and state agencies. Many also offer their members insurance and other benefits and have useful publications.

Small Business Administration

The U.S. Small Business Administration, or SBA, is an independent federal agency that helps small businesses. The SBA is best known for providing loan guaranties to bolster small businesses that want to start or expand, but it provides several other useful services for small businesses, including:

- **SBA Answer Desk.** The Answer Desk is a nationwide, toll-free information center that helps callers with questions and problems about starting and running businesses. Service is provided through a computerized telephone message system augmented by staff counselors. It is available 24 hours a day, seven days a week, with counselors available Monday through Friday, 9 am to 5 pm Eastern Time. The Answer Desk can be reached at 800-8-ASK-SBA.

- **Publications.** The SBA also produces and maintains a library of publications, videos, and computer programs. These are available by mail to SBA customers for a nominal fee. A complete listing of these products is in the Resource Directory for Small Business Management. SBA field offices also offer free publications that describe SBA programs and services.

- **SBA Internet site (www.sba.gov).** You can download SBA publications from the SBA Internet site and obtain information about SBA programs and services, points of contact, and calendars of local events. The Internet address is www.sba.gov.

- **SCORE program.** The Service Corps of Retired Executives, or SCORE, is a group of retired business people who volunteer to help others in business. To find a SCORE chapter in your area, visit the SCORE website at www.score.org, or call the national SCORE office at 800-634-0245.

The SBA has offices in all major cities. Look in the phone book under U.S. Government for the office nearest you.

Online Small Business Resources

The online world includes the Internet, commercial online services such as America Online and CompuServe, and specialized computer databases such as Westlaw and Lexis. All contain useful information for the computer-savvy self-employed.

Internet Resources

There are hundreds of Internet sites dealing with small business issues, such as starting a small business, marketing, and business opportunities. Beware, however, that no one checks these sites for accuracy. A good way to find these sites is through an Internet directory such as Yahoo. You can access Yahoo at www.yahoo.com. Click on the Business and Economy category and then on the Small Business Information listing. A few particularly useful websites for self-employed people include:

- the CCH Business Owner's Toolkit (www.toolkit.cch.com)
- the Quicken small business website (www.quicken.com/small_business)
- the Yahoo Small Business Center (http://smallbusiness.yahoo.com)
- the Small Business Taxes & Management website (www.smbiz.com).

A growing number of court decisions are also available on the Internet for free or at nominal cost. You can find a comprehensive set of links to free case law websites at www.findlaw.com. You can also obtain legal decisions from the subscription websites www.westlaw.com and www.lexis.com.

Nolo Internet Site

Nolo maintains an Internet site that is useful for the self-employed. The site contains helpful articles, information about new legislation, book excerpts, and the Nolo catalog. The site also includes a legal encyclopedia with specific information for people who are self-employed, as well as a legal research center you can use to find state and federal statutes. The Internet address is www.nolo.com.

Commercial Online Services

Some of the best known parts of the online world are commercial online services such as CompuServe and America Online. To access these systems, a person must become a subscriber and pay a monthly (and sometimes hourly) fee. These systems typically offer online chats with other users logged onto the system, posting of public messages on various topics, and vast collections of electronic databases. All of these services have special areas devoted to small business owners and consultants. For example, MSN has Bcentral, CompuServe has a Working at Home Forum, and America Online has a Small Business area. You can also obtain information on taxes and download copies of IRS tax forms.

State Offices Providing Small Business Help

Below we provide a listing of state offices that can assist small businesses.

Alabama

Economic and Community Affairs
401 Adams Avenue
P.O. Box 5690
Montgomery, AL 36130
800-248-0033*; 205-242-0400
www.alalinc.net/partner.
cfm?Location=secretary

*In-state calling only.

Alaska

Division of Community and Business
  Development
Department of Community and
  Economic Development
P.O. Box 110809
Juneau, AK 99811-0804
907-465-2017
www.dced.state.ak.us/cbd

Arizona

Department of Commerce
3800 North Central Avenue
Suite 1500
Phoenix, AZ 85012
602-280-1300
www.az.gov/webapp/portal/topic.
  ysp?id=1158

Arkansas

Small Business Information Center
Industrial Development Commission
State Capitol Mall
Room 4C-300
Little Rock, AR 72201
501-682-5275
www.sosweb.state.ar.us

California

Office of Small Business
Department of Commerce
801 K Street, Suite 1700
Sacramento, CA 95814
916-327-4357; 916-445-6545
www.ss.ca.gov/business/business.htm

Colorado

Economic Development Commission
1625 Broadway, Suite 1700
Denver, CO 80202
303-892-3725
www.state.co.us/gov_dir/sos/index.
  html

Connecticut

Department of Economic and
Community Development
505 Hudson Street
Hartford, CT 06106
203-258-4200
www.state.ct.us/ecd

Delaware

Development Office
P.O. Box 1401
99 Kings Highway
Dover, DE 19903
302-739-4271
www.state.de.us/corp/index.htm

District of Columbia

Office of Business and Economic
  Development
Twelfth Floor
717 14th Street NW
Washington, DC 20005
202-727-6600
www.dcra.org

Florida

Bureau of Business Assistance
Department of Commerce
107 West Gaines Street, Room 443
Tallahassee, FL 32399-2000
800-342-0771*; 904-488-9357
www.dos.state.fl.us/doc/index.html

Georgia

Department of Community Affairs
100 Peachtree Street, Suite 1200
Atlanta, GA 30303
404-656-6200
www.sos.state.ga.us/corporations

Hawaii

Small Business Information Service
2404 Maile Way
Room A 202
University of Hawaii
Honolulu, HI 96819
808-956-7363
www.hawaii.gov/dbedt/index.html

Idaho

Economic Development Division
Department of Commerce
700 W. State Street
Boise, ID 83720-0093
208-334-2470
www.idsos.state.id.us/corp/corindex.
htm

Illinois

Department of Commerce and
Community Affairs
620 East Adams Street
Springfield, IL 62701
800-252-2923*; 217-782-3235
www.commerce.state.il.us/bus/index.
html

Indiana

Ombudsman's Office
Community Development Division
Department of Commerce
One North Capitol, Suite 700

Indianapolis, IN 46204-2288
800-824-2476*; 317-232-8891
www.state.in.us/sos/bus_service

Iowa

Bureau of Small Business
  Development
Department of Economic
  Development
200 East Grand Avenue
Des Moines, IA 50309
800-532-1216*; 515-242-4720
www.sos.state.ia.us

Kansas

Division of Existing Industry
Development
700 SW Harrison, Suite 1300
Topeka, KN 66603
913-296-2741
www.kssos.org

Kentucky

Division of Small Business
2400 Capitol Plaza Tower
Frankfort, KY 40601
800-626-2250*; 502-564-7670
www.sos.state.ky.us

Louisiana

Department of Economic
  Development
Office of Commerce and Industry
P.O. Box 94185
Baton Rouge, LA 70804-9185
504-342-5365
www.lded.state.la.us

*In-state calling only.

Maine

Business Development Division
Department of Economic and
 Community Development
State House 59
187 State Street
Augusta, ME 04333
800-872-3838*; 207-287-2656
www.state.me.us/sos/cec/cec.htm

Maryland

Division of Business Development
Department of Economic and
 Employment Development
217 East Redwood Street
Baltimore, MD 21202
800-873-7232; 410-767-3316
www.dat.state.md.us

Massachusetts

Office of Business Development
1 Ashburton Place, Room 301
Boston, MA 02202
617-727-8380
www.state.ma.us/sec/cor/coridx.htm

Michigan

Michigan Jobs Commission
Ombudsman's Office
201 N. Washington Square
Lansing, MI 48913
517-373-9808
www.michigan.gov/emi/1,1303,7-102-
 115—,00.html

Minnesota

Small Business Assistance Office
Department of Trade and Economic
 Development

500 Metro Square Building
121 E. 7th Place
Street Paul, MN 55101-2146
800-652-9747; 651-297-9706
www.sos.state.mn.us/business/index.
 html

Mississippi

Mississippi Development Authority
P.O. Box 849
Jackson, MS 39205
601-359-3349
www.ms.gov/frameset.jsp?URL=http%
 3A%2F%2fwww.mississippi.org%2F

Missouri

Small Business Development Center
300 University Place
Columbia, MO 65211
573-882-0344
http://mosl.sos.state.mo.us

Montana

Business Assistance Division
Department of Commerce
1218 Sixth Street
Helena, MT 59601
800-221-8015*; 406-444-3797
www.state.mt.us/sos/biz.htm

Nebraska

Existing Business Division
Department of Economic Development
P.O. Box 94666
301 Centennial Mall South
Lincoln, NE 68509-4666
402-471-3747
www.nol.org/home/SOS/htm/services.
 htm

*In-state calling only.

Nevada

Nevada Commission on Economic
  Development
Capitol Complex
5151 S. Carson Street
Carson City, NV 89710
702-687-4325
http://sos.state.nv.us

New Hampshire

Small Business Development Center
108 McConnell Hall
University of New Hampshire
15 College Road
Durham, NH 03824
603-862-2200
www.state.nh.us/agency/agencies.html

New Jersey

Office of Small Business Assistance
Department of Commerce and
  Economic Growth Commission
20 West State Street, CN 835
Trenton, NJ 08625
609-292-2444
www.state.nj.us/njbgs/services.html

New Mexico

Economic Division
Department of Economic
  Development
1100 Street Francis Drive
P.O. Box 20003
Santa Fe, NM 87503
505-827-0300
www.edd.state.nm.us/about.htm

New York

Division for Small Business
Department of Economic
  Development
1515 Broadway
51st Floor
New York, NY 10036
212-827-6150
www.dos.state.ny.us/corp/corpwww.
  html

North Carolina

Business and Industry Division
Department of Commerce
Dobbs Building, Room 2019
430 North Salisbury Street
Raleigh, NC 27611
919-733-4151
www.ncgov.com/asp/basic/business.
  asp

North Dakota

Small Business Coordinator
Economic Development Commission
1833 E. Bismark Expressway
Bismark, ND 58504
701-328-5300
www.state.nd.us/sec

Ohio

Small and Developing Business
  Division
Department of Development
77 S. High Street
Columbus, OH 43215
800-248-4040*; 614-466-4232
www.state.oh.us/sos

*In-state calling only.

Oklahoma

Oklahoma Department of Commerce
P.O. Box 26980
6601 N. Broadway Extension
Oklahoma City, OK 73126-0980
800-477-6552*; 405-843-9770
www.state.ok.us

Oregon

Economic Development Department
775 Summer Street NE
Salem, OR 97310
800-233-3306*; 503-986-0110
www.sos.state.or.us/corporation/
    corphp.htm

Pennsylvania

Bureau of Small Business and
    Appalachian Development
    Department of Commerce
461 Forum Building
Harrisburg, PA 17120
717-783-5700
www.dos.state.pa.us/corp/corp.htm

Rhode Island

Business Development Division
Department of Economic
    Development
Seven Jackson Walkway
Providence, RI 02903
401-277-2601
www.sec.state.ri.us/submenus/
    buslink.htm

South Carolina

Enterprise Development
P.O. Box 1149
Columbia, SC 29202
803-252-8806
www.callsouthcarolina.com

South Dakota

Governor's Office of Economic
    Development
Capital Lake Plaza
711 Wells Avenue
Pierre, SD 57501
800-872-6190*; 605-773-5032
www.sdgreatprofits.com

Tennessee

Small Business Office
Department of Economic and
    Community Development
320 Sixth Avenue North
Eighth Floor
Rachel Jackson Building
Nashville, TN 37219
800-872-7201*; 615-741-1888
www.state.tn.us/sos/service.htm

Texas

Small Business Division
Department of Commerce
Economic Development Commission
P.O. Box 12728
Capitol Station
410 East Fifth Street
Austin, TX 78711
800-888-0511; 512-936-0100
www.tded.state.tx.us/smallbusiness

*In-state calling only.

Utah

Division of Business and Economic
Development
324 South State Street, 5th Floor
Salt Lake City, UT 84114
801-538-8700
www.utah.org/dbcd/welcome.htm

Vermont

Agency of Development and
Community Affairs
The Pavilion
109 State Street
Montpelier, VT 05609
800-622-4553*; 802-828-3221
www.sec.state.vt.us/corps/corpindex.
htm

Virginia

Small Business and Financial Services
Department of Economic
Development
P.O. Box 798
1021 E. Cary Street
11th Floor
Richmond, VA 23206-0798
804-371-8106
www.state.va.us/scc/division/clk/
index.htm

Washington

Small Business Development Center
Krugel Hall, Room 135

Washington State University
Pullman, WA 99164-4727
509-335-1576
www.secstate.wa.gov/corps/default.
htm

West Virginia

Economic Development Authority
1018 Kanawha Boulevard E., Suite 501
Charleston, WV 25301
304-558-3650
www.state.wv.us/sos

Wisconsin

Department of Commerce
201 West Washington Avenue
Madison, WI 53717
608-266-1018
www.commerce.state.wi.us

Wyoming

Economic and Community
Development Division
Commerce Department
6101 Yellowstone Road
Cheyenne, WY 82002
307-777-7284
http://soswy.state.wy.us/corporat/
corporat.htm

Source: National Association for the Self-
Employed, *USA TODAY* research, updated
by Nolo.

■

*In-state calling only.

Index

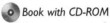

Remember:

Little publishers have big ears.
We really listen to you.

Take 2 Minutes & Give Us Your 2 cents

Your comments make a big difference in the development and revision of Nolo books and software. Please take a few minutes and register your Nolo product—and your comments—with us. Not only will your input make a difference, you'll receive special offers available only to registered owners of Nolo products on our newest books and software. Register now by:

PHONE
1-800-728-3555

FAX
1-800-645-0895

EMAIL
cs@nolo.com

or **MAIL** us
this registration card

fold here

Registration Card

NAME _____ DATE _____

ADDRESS _____

_____

CITY _____ STATE _____ ZIP _____

PHONE _____ EMAIL _____

WHERE DID YOU HEAR ABOUT THIS PRODUCT? _____

WHERE DID YOU PURCHASE THIS PRODUCT? _____

DID YOU CONSULT A LAWYER? (PLEASE CIRCLE ONE)   YES   NO   NOT APPLICABLE

DID YOU FIND THIS BOOK HELPFUL?   (VERY)   5   4   3   2   1   (NOT AT ALL)

COMMENTS _____

_____

_____

WAS IT EASY TO USE?   (VERY EASY)   5   4   3   2   1   (VERY DIFFICULT)

We occasionally make our mailing list available to carefully selected companies whose products may be of interest to you.

❏ If you do not wish to receive mailings from these companies, please check this box.

❏ You can quote me in future Nolo promotional materials.
Daytime phone number _____.

FINA 1.0

Nolo in the NEWS

"Nolo helps lay people perform legal tasks without the aid—or fees—of lawyers."

—USA TODAY

Nolo books are ..."written in plain language, free of legal mumbo jumbo, and spiced with witty personal observations."*

—ASSOCIATED PRESS

"...Nolo publications...guide people simply through the how, when, where and why of law."

—WASHINGTON POST

"Increasingly, people who are not lawyers are performing tasks usually regarded as legal work... And consumers, using books like Nolo's, do routine legal work themselves."

—NEW YORK TIMES

"...All of [Nolo's] books are easy-to-understand, are updated regularly, provide pull-out forms...and are often quite moving in their sense of compassion for the struggles of the lay reader."

—SAN FRANCISCO CHRONICLE

fold here

- -

Nolo
950 Parker Street
Berkeley, CA 94710-9867

Attn: FINA 1.0